T0024520

Mahamudra

Mahamudra

How to Discover Our True Nature

LAMA THUBTEN YESHE

Edited by Robina Courtin

Wisdom

Wisdom Publications, Inc.
199 Elm Street
Somerville MA 02144 USA
wisdompubs.org

© 2018 Lama Yeshe Wisdom Archive
All rights reserved.

No part of this book may be reproduced in any form or by any means,
electronic or mechanical, including photography, recording, or by any
information storage and retrieval system or technologies now known or
later developed, without permission in writing from the publisher.

Library of Congress Cataloging-in-Publication Data
Names: Thubten Yeshe, 1935–1984, author. | Blo-bzang-chos-kyi-rgyal-
    mtshan, Panchen Lama I, 1570–1662. | Courtin, Robina, editor.
Title: Mahamudra: how to discover our true nature / Lama
    Thubten Yeshe; edited by Robina Courtin.
Description: Somerville, MA: Wisdom Publications, Inc., 2018. | Includes index. |
Identifiers: LCCN 2017057636 (print) | LCCN 2017061205 (ebook) |
    ISBN 9781614294108 (ebook) | ISBN 9781614293958 (pbk.: alk. paper) |
Subjects: LCSH: Mahamudra (Tantric rite) | Dge-lugs-pa
    (Sect)—Rituals. | Bka-brgyud-pa (Sect)—Rituals.
Classification: LCC BQ8921.M35 (ebook) | LCC BQ8921.
    M35 T49 2018 (print) | DDC 294.3/4435—dc23
LC record available at https://lccn.loc.gov/2017057636

ISBN 978-1-61429-395-8   ebook ISBN 978-1-61429-410-8

22 21 20 19 18
5 4 3 2 1

Cover design by Gopa & Ted 2. Interior design by Kristin Goble.
Set in Diacritical Garamond Pro 11/16.

Wisdom Publications' books are printed on acid-free paper and meet the
guidelines for permanence and durability of the Production Guidelines
for Book Longevity of the Council on Library Resources.

♻ This book was produced with environmental mindfulness. For more
information, please visit wisdompubs.org/wisdom-environment.

Printed in the United States of America.

Contents

Editor's Preface

Lama Thubten Yeshe (1935–84) gave instructions on maha-mudra meditation to seventy of his students during a two-week retreat in the Australian winter of 1981, August 2–15. The host was Atisha Centre, situated on fifty acres of flat, low-growing bushland just west of the small town of Eaglehawk, ninety miles north of Melbourne in the southeastern state of Victoria. The property had been offered to Lama Yeshe's Foundation for the Preservation of the Mahayana Tradition (FPMT) earlier that year by the father of Ian Green, one of the students.

Nothing had been built yet, so the retreat was held in a little wooden church next door, in Sandhurst Town, a replica of a village from the mid-nineteenth-century Victorian gold-rush era run by the Green family for tourists. Volunteers did a complete renovation of the church's interior in time for the event.

Lama paid homage to "the great Indian yogi" Atisha and to an "Australian Atisha":

> Atisha Centre has an auspicious name. The great Indian yogi Atisha (982–1054), who taught in Tibet during the later years of his life, was successful in his mahamudra practice; he discovered his own mahamudra. From the Tibetan point of view, Atisha was a buddha, an enlightened one.

Lama Yeshe in Sandhurst Town, before the retreat.
Lama's casual style belies
the fact that he was a scholar and a yogi.

This place has the energy of this yogi as well as the energy of an Australian Atisha, the man who offered this facility. He is not Buddhist, but in his heart maybe he is.

The instructions from that two-week retreat form the bulk of this book, supplemented with advice Lama gave at retreats hosted by two of his own FPMT centers, Vajrapani Institute in California in 1977 and Maitreya Instituut in Amsterdam in 1981. Nine months after the Atisha Centre event, in March 1982, Lama also gave advice in India during the first Enlightened Experience Celebration, a marvelous festival of teachings, empowerments, and retreats spanning six months. Organized by Lama Yeshe especially for his Western students—hundreds attended—many of the teachings and empowerments were given by his own gurus, including His Holiness the Dalai Lama.

He had requested His Holiness to give a commentary on the same text that he himself had used at Atisha Centre, the First Panchen Lama Losang Chokyi Gyaltsen's *Highway of the Conquerors: The Mahamudra Root Text of the Precious Genden Oral Tradition.* (This commentary has since been edited by Alexander Berzin, who translated for His Holiness at the event, and incorporated with other teachings and published as *The Gelug/Kagyü Tradition of Mahamudra.*)

At the retreat, Lama Yeshe explained that mahamudra is a name given to "the universal reality of emptiness, of nonduality"—

> the inborn nature of all phenomena. It exists equally in all things: organic, nonorganic, permanent, impermanent, including all beings....
>
> Perhaps you're thinking that if mahamudra is about emptiness, then you have heard it many times before. You're right; the teachings are not so different. But the unique approach of this presentation is the emphasis on meditation—the *experience* of emptiness rather than explaining what it means.

In mahamudra meditation, Lama says, the object of concentration is our own mind, in particular its clarity, its conventional nature. And, as His Holiness says in his commentary, finally the goal is to realize the emptiness of the mind, its ultimate nature.

If we explain in terms of the [middle way] tradition of a correct view of reality, the usual method for gaining correct understanding is to realize the emptiness of a person—a conventional "me." For this, we analyze the mode of existence of a person in terms of the five aggregates as the basis for labeling one. . . .

In the mahamudra tradition, however, although we still take as the basis for labeling a person the five aggregates, we focus primarily on the aggregate of consciousness as serving this function. Thus the mahamudra tradition presents a correct view of reality in terms of the emptiness of the mind.

First, however, it's necessary to realize the emptiness of one's self. Lama Yeshe says to start by focusing on the thoughts: whatever arises in our mind. When the consciousness settles, we focus on its clarity. Once there is a reasonable level of concentration, in order to recognize that there is no independent self, the Panchen Lama says to "investigate intelligently with subtle awareness the essence of the individual who is meditating, just like a small fish that moves in lucid waters without causing any disturbance."

In his commentary, His Holiness explains the next step:

Once we have gained conviction in the lack of true and inherent identity on the basis of our own self, we turn to . . . other phenomena. . . .

As part of this process, we now take mind as the basis for emptiness—in other words, as the basis that is empty of existing in any fantasized and impossible way. We scrutinize and analyze mind with a correct view to gain a decisive understanding of its empty nature.

Throughout the retreat, many of the teachings were given as guided meditations, with Lama emphasizing the experience of emptiness of one's self. He inspired students to go beyond ego's addiction to a limited sense of self and to taste the lightness and expansiveness of their own mind, their own very being. As always, his words are not only experiential but also direct, funny, deceptively simple, and incredibly encouraging—enlightenment seems possible. And, as always, in his desire to counteract a tendency in contemporary society to mystify meditation, he brings the instructions right down to earth, making them doable even by beginners. He goes to incredible lengths to explain the meaning of what would otherwise remain merely intellectual or arcane.

And there is no limit to Lama's creativity in finding ways to do this. For example, he uses twenty-one different terms for "affliction," the main term used in Buddhist psychology—which he *doesn't* use!—to refer to states of mind such as attachment, anger, and the primordial clinging to an independent self. Some of the terms are variations of accepted synonyms, but most are his own creation: artificial concept, confused thoughts, contradictory concept, delusion, deluded thought, dualistic concept, dualistic puzzle, dualistic thought, fanatical thinking, fantasy, hallucination, hallucinated projection, hallucinated vision, impure concept, limited concept, misconception, mistaken concept, negative mental energy, projection, superstition, wrong conception.

His easygoing style and casual words belie the reality that he was a scholar, but they are, perhaps, evidence that he was also a yogi, a knowledge-holder (in Tibetan, *rigzin*). It all sounds so simple because he is speaking from his own direct experience.

At the end of the retreat Lama gave the students a taste of mahamudra from the perspective of tantra, in keeping with the tradition of the lineage lamas, all of whom, he says, became enlightened by practicing it.

And as a prerequisite for this level of practice, an empowerment into the highest yoga tantra practice of Heruka Chakrasamvara was given before the teachings, a first in Australia.

If you want to know more about tantric mahamudra, you can read Lama Yeshe's *Bliss of Inner Fire*. And because deity yoga is a crucial component of this approach to mahamudra, you can also study his *Becoming the Compassion Buddha* and the e-book *Universal Love: The Yoga Method of Buddha Maitreya*. Lama also gives tantric teachings in his bestselling *Introduction to Tantra*, in *Becoming Vajrasattva*, and elsewhere in the vast online resources available at the Lama Yeshe Wisdom Archive.

Lama Yeshe's main disciple, Lama Thubten Zopa Rinpoche—who took over the spiritual direction of the FPMT after Lama passed away in March, 1984—has said about his guru:

> He was a great tantric practitioner, a real ascetic meditator, even though he didn't live alone in a cave. Lama was a great hidden yogi. He was a valid base to be labeled "yogi," not because he could perform tantric rituals but because he had unmistaken realizations of clear light and the illusory body. He had reached the stage of tantra mahamudra.

On August 14, the day before the retreat ended, Lama invited Ian Green and another student, Garrey Foulkes, to come for a walk with him around Atisha Centre's undeveloped acres. As if he were already familiar with the place, Lama led the way to a gentle hill in the mainly flat bushland and announced that this was the site for a *big* stupa—a representation of enlightened mind—with a *big* meditation hall inside. Motioning to spots in the bush nearby, he said *here* will be a village for laypeople and *there* a hospice. Finally, leading Ian and Garrey to another hill, Lama declared that here there will be a monastery.

Thirty-seven years later the entire area is flourishing. Atisha Centre runs Tibetan Buddhist courses and retreats year-round. Thubten Shedrup Ling Monastery is a beautiful environment for up to twenty monks, and a place for nuns—Machig Labdron Nunnery—has been established as well.

Plans are in place for the development of the Lama Yeshe Village, an aged-care facility including hospice services, as well as a primary school, a hotel, a restaurant, and other facilities.

Finally, the grand centerpiece of Lama Yeshe's vision, the Great Stupa of Universal Compassion, a replica of the fifteenth-century edifice in Gyantse, Tibet—with, indeed, "a big meditation hall inside," which can hold two thousand people—is well under way. A decades-long project, it is the biggest stupa in the Western world (stupa.org.au).

I'm grateful to Yangsi Rinpoche of Maitripa College in Portland, Oregon, in the United States and Geshe Loden of Institut Vajra Yogini near Toulouse in France for clarifying some points. Thanks to Norma Quesada for checking the transcript of Lama Yeshe's words and her initial editing—so helpful. Thanks also to Wisdom's David Kittelstrom and Daniel Aitken and his team for their enthusiasm; Nicholas Ribush and Gordon McDougall of Lama Yeshe Wisdom Archive; Voula Zarpani for her translation of the Panchen Lama's text; Marije van de Vlekkert for her reworking of the seventeenth-century woodblock print of the Panchen Lama reproduced on page 12; and François Lecointre and Violette Pliot-Lecointre for offering me, year after year, the blessed space of Institut Vajra Yogini to work in.

Robina Courtin

PART 1

Preparing for Mahamudra

I

Mahamudra Is
Beyond Words

The Great Seal: Emptiness

According to Tibetan Buddhism, mahamudra is one of the most advanced teachings of the Buddha. *Mahamudra* is Sanskrit: *maha* means "great" and *mudra* can be translated as "seal." When you lend me one hundred dollars, we make a contract and we seal it, don't we? It shows: "Next year I have the obligation to pay you back." You have the document as a guarantee.

However, *this* seal, this great seal, is not a physical seal made in a factory. It is the universal reality of emptiness, non-duality, non–self-existence. It exists in all phenomena, including sentient beings. It is also not some made-up philosophical concept. It doesn't matter whether you accept it or deny it. If I say, "I don't believe there is an earth; I don't believe there is a sun," who cares? Even though I reject the existence of the sun,

I'm standing in the rays of the sun. Even though I deny the existence of the earth, I'm standing on the earth.

The reality of nonduality is inescapable. It is the inborn nature of all phenomena. It exists equally in all things: organic, nonorganic, permanent, impermanent, including all beings. It exists always within us. The name we give it is *mahamudra*.

Mahamudra Brings You Beyond Fear

The trouble is we totally believe in *exactly* the opposite of nonduality. We grasp at a dualistic me—a self-existent, real, separate me. We've been grasping at it since we were in our mother's womb—actually, the belief in this simultaneously born ego has been with us since beginningless time. It's beyond intellectual. Even ants and dogs have it. And as the great Mahayana scholar Dharmakirti points out, this primordial belief in a separate "me" creates the concept of "other." From this tremendous gap comes the evolution of all of samsara, the cycle of existence.

To knock out this hallucinated vision, we must realize mahamudra, nonduality. The realization of mahamudra cuts the wrong conceptions and destroys the nuclear energy of ego. This is revolutionary—more revolutionary than any political ideology. And it brings you totally beyond fear: mahamudra is the antidote to fear. So beautiful!

Mahamudra Is Beyond Words

In mahamudra meditation there is no doctrine, no theology, no philosophy, no God, no Buddha. We go beyond name, beyond shape and color, beyond the relative, beyond self-image, beyond compassion. With our own consciousness we can experience the universal, infinity. We can just *be* in the experience of totality.

Using Buddhist terminology, we say that mahamudra is beyond arising and beyond cessation. Mahamudra is only *experience*. The moment I say words, you interpret them in this way or that, and then it becomes a problem. So don't trust my words—they are the false words of my superstition; Buddhism thinks that way. No matter what words I say, they still come from my conceptions. You have to go beyond words.

We also say that mahamudra has no dimension, no distinct nature, and no cause or effect. Remember, when Shakyamuni Buddha discovered enlightenment, he was silent for several weeks; he felt it was not possible to express the deep, universal mahamudra experience to others. Such profound things cannot be explained to anyone who hasn't reached that stage.

Two Approaches to Realizing Emptiness

Perhaps you're thinking that if mahamudra is about emptiness, then you have heard it many times before. You're right; the teachings are not so different. But the unique approach of this presentation is the emphasis on meditation—the *experience* of emptiness rather than explaining what it means.

In the mahamudra root text I am using here, Panchen Lama Losang Chokyi Gyaltsen says there are two approaches to realizing emptiness:

> Between the two approaches of (1) seeking meditation [on calm abiding] on the basis of the view and (2) seeking the view on the basis of meditation [on calm abiding], the explanation here follows the second approach.

We usually hear that Lama Je Tsongkhapa, founder of our Gelug lineage, says that first we should study, then analyze, then meditate. In other words, we should "seek meditation on the basis of the view." But Panchen Lama, one of the Gelugpas' foremost figures and an expert in Lama Tsongkhapa's tradition, is saying here that we can meditate first, *then* seek mahamudra, emptiness. We can "seek the view on the basis of meditation."

Which is right? Well, both are right. But here we are following the second approach.

The First Approach: Learn About Emptiness First, Then Meditate

We used the first approach when I studied in the monastery. We read so much, memorizing and reciting and debating philosophical texts every day. Buddhist philosophy is so sophisticated, so intellectual, involving highly complex thinking. I thought that if I understood all the philosophy, the middle way, everything, I'd knock out the ego. I thought about that a lot. I checked, checked, checked—and then I realized my conception was not true. I was shocked! I realized that even if I knew all the Buddhist texts and understood them intellectually, it would never touch my heart unless I meditated.

When we learn the words alone, there is no satisfaction; the problem of ego is not solved. And now I look at many of my students: they read so many books! All the philosophy, the psychology, so much information. All this reading, reading, reading!

Of course, with this approach we must also meditate. Lama Tsongkhapa talks about the union of the three wisdoms that arise from hearing, analyzing, and meditating; in Tibetan we say *trojung*, *sangjung*, and *gomjung*. But people sometimes misinterpret this. They hear that we Gelugpas study for twenty or thirty years and think it means that first you listen for twenty years, then check for another twenty years, then, finally, penetrate in meditation. In fact, from the beginning we integrate these three wisdoms—we practice them simultaneously—and at each stage of our development it's a question of proportion.

Nevertheless, there is the danger that your knowledge will remain merely intellectual. If you don't go beyond the intellectual level, your mind will not be transformed. It's as if the knowledge stays in the books and you are separate from it. You can never get rid of ego this way. You end up missing the point.

The Second Approach: Meditate First, Then Discover Emptiness

It is extremely difficult to knock out the ego. You cannot seek the ego's projections philosophically, with your intellect. When you practice mahamudra, intellect is the enemy. You have to go beyond the intellect—you have to meditate. Then real transformation can come.

We have to understand, Buddha Maitreya said, that the relative Dharma, everything in the books, is like a bridge. A bridge is helpful for crossing a river, but once you've crossed it, it's "Goodbye bridge!" isn't it? You have to touch the heart. Once you've experienced the fundamental nature of your own self—and your own consciousness—it's goodbye to all the philosophical concepts.

Philosophy is the equipment we use to reach *beyond* the bondage, but still it is bondage, isn't it? I'm not trying to be revolutionary! Of course, the philosophy is *good*; it is unbelievably profound, we should respect it. But we are seekers, and we can make mistakes. We can interpret the teachings wrongly. So we need to develop the skill to go *beyond* philosophy. We should not be afraid to go beyond it!

When the great yogis Milarepa and Lama Tsongkhapa went into retreat in the mountains, they didn't bring their books with them; they went beyond scripture, beyond ink, beyond Parker pens. And even as a boy, Lama Tsongkhapa meditated and communicated directly with Manjushri, the buddha of wisdom. So it is definitely possible first to meditate and then discover emptiness. This is the approach here.

Mahamudra is a super, incredible method. This is the experience of the lineage lamas, all the great yogis and yoginis. They all realized mahamudra in meditation.

Your Wisdom Will Explode

When you've escaped the bondage of the intellect and touched reality, you experience an explosion of knowledge. In this state you have infinitely more space in your mind and can learn many things effortlessly. You will be amazed. "Wow! I didn't know I had that much knowledge! What happened?"

Normally you are bound up tightly in your superstitions. If these are released, you can touch an unbelievable dimension of reality. Without expecting it, you suddenly, without effort, realize things; you *know*. This is possible, I tell you; it's not some Tibetan religious fantasy.

Milarepa is a good example. He didn't study any philosophy, but because of his mahamudra meditation he had gained total understanding of all dimensions of reality. The intellectuals, who'd studied for years and years, would come to debate with him, and he always knew the answers. He blew their minds!

They'd ask him, "Do you know Vinaya?" This subject, which covers all the vows for monks and nuns, has so much detail, is so sophisticated, so complicated, and in the monastery we study and debate it for at least four years.

"No!" said Milarepa. "I don't know anything about Vinaya, non-Vinaya! If my mind is subdued, if I conquer my ego and touch universal reality, that's *my* Vinaya." The Tibetan word for Vinaya is *dulwa*, and it means "to subdue the mind." His answer is super!

When I was a boy, I really liked Milarepa. Reading about his life was so helpful; it gave me unbelievable inspiration. You, too, should read his life story. It will give you tremendous energy.

Not Seeing Is the Perfect Seeing

In Tibetan, we have this saying of the Buddha: "Not seeing is the perfect seeing." "My goodness!" you may be thinking, "This mahamudra is strange!" For experienced meditators these words are super profound. They refer to the *experience* of mahamudra; the experience of universal reality, nonduality.

Let's say that a Tibetan monk comes to your Western country. He opens his sense perceptions to the West. Meaning well, you want to share with him those experiences you find pleasurable, so you take him to the beach. "You Tibetans have seen only rocks and mountains. Here, look how beautiful the sea is!" you say. "On the mountain, you can't see fish; here there are so many fish. And people without clothes." Well, okay, maybe my example has gone far enough! I think I'm getting carried away now; I have to control!

For the poor Tibetan monk, then, maybe seeing all these new things is too much. Perhaps *not* seeing is the best. *Not* seeing, *not* perceiving dualistic phenomena, is the perfect seeing, the perfect experience.

You understand now. When the object is not there, the concept can't be there. Object and subject operate together.

When we experience mahamudra, dualistic phenomena no longer operate. When the object breaks down, the concept, the subject, disappears. You don't need to push. Buddhist teachings work so peacefully. It's so scientific, so experiential. So, *not* looking at the dualistic complex situation and instead having the experience of nonduality is the perfect view.

All conventional phenomena are so relative, so changeable, so artificial, so momentary. Our concepts are so fast, the superstitions are so fast, the relative world is so fast. Why? Because according to Buddhism this is a time when superstition is exploding—and the superstitious mind is the resource of the revolutionary change of conventional reality. The problem is ego holding every changing thing as absolute. We need to cut the concept of ego and thereby discover nonduality. We *can* do it, all right?

The not-seeing of dualistic puzzles is the seeing of perfection, unity, totality. The more we realize this, the more integrated we become, and the less we put ourselves in disordered situations. For this we need tremendous renunciation. We must become flexible; we must learn to let go.

We Will Meditate

So let's try to make these teachings experiential. Let's meditate. Actually, sometimes my Tibetan friends criticize me for teaching meditation to Westerners. "They should study for twenty years first, just like you did," they tell me. But I don't care!

Panchen Lama Losang Chokyi Gyaltsen

2

The Lineage of Mahamudra

At First, Mahamudra Was Kept Secret

When the great Indian yogi Atisha was alive in Tibet in the eleventh century, and even later in the early fifteenth century when Lama Tsongkhapa was around, mahamudra was not taught publicly. There were no books in the name of mahamudra; it was kept secret. But there was an oral tradition: the instructions were passed on by the lama directly to the rare student who was ready.

Later, in the seventeenth century, it was the First Panchen Lama, Losang Chokyi Gyaltsen, who first wrote these instructions down on paper. He had received the teachings from his guru Sangye Yeshe. We Gelugpas now use these instructions as our root text, and, as I mentioned, I am using them here. When you read the text (in part 4), you will see the value of it.

The Lineages of Mahamudra

These mahamudra teachings have been passed down to us through various lineages. We don't have time to go through everything in detail—anyway, I'd rather use our time for meditation—so I will discuss this only briefly.

One way has them passing from Vajradhara to Vajrapani, then to the great Indian Mahayana saints such as Nagarjuna, Chandrakirti, eventually Tilopa, Naropa, Tibet's Marpa, Atisha, and finally Tsongkhapa. This is the *long lineage*. According to Tibetan Buddhism all these lineage yogis discovered enlightenment in their lifetime by practicing mahamudra according to highest yoga tantra.

Another way to present the transmission is what we call the *close lineage*. Shakyamuni Buddha passed the teachings to Manjushri, and Lama Tsongkhapa communicated directly with Manjushri, receiving the technical meditation instructions from him. Tsongkhapa passed on his experiences to his disciple Togden Jampal Gyatso, who shared them with Baso Chokyi Gyaltsen, who in turn gave them to the mahasiddha Chokyi Dorje. The great yogi Ensapa received them from Chokyi Dorje and transmitted them to the Panchen Lama's guru, Sangye Yeshe, who then passed on the instructions to his disciple. You can find the stories of their lives translated into English.

Since then, these teachings have been passed down in an unbroken lineage of holy beings to the present day. I think they, too, all reached enlightenment in that one lifetime by practicing mahamudra.

You, Too, Can Achieve Mahamudra

I first received the teachings on mahamudra when I was twenty-one or twenty-two, three years or so before we escaped to India in 1959. Remember, that was when the Chinese said to us Tibetans, "Go away!" During that month of teachings, I became really inspired hearing about all the lineage lamas, the great yogis, and how they experienced mahamudra. The teachings became real for me. I thought, "These meditators were ordinary human beings who reached higher realizations," so I decided I can do it too. I became ambitious. You understand? I felt so much inspiration: "It is possible. It can be done."

Looking at the historical facts about the lives of these enlightened ones was so helpful, so encouraging. We shouldn't read only philosophy. We need to look at the actual human experiences of these great beings; this is good research. We come to see that their realizations aren't something outrageous, something impossible to achieve. No.

These are real success stories. These yogis were successful spiritually. And, before that, they were successful materially as well. It's not as if they were hippies beforehand. No! If we look at Shakyamuni Buddha's history, we'll see that first he had a rich samsara. He had a kingdom; more than the entire wealth of a big city belonged to him. And then, at a certain point, he threw off his dualistic robes and disappeared into nothingness. It was the same for Milarepa, same for Tilopa, Naropa, Tsongkhapa.

Lama Tsongkhapa had thousands of devoted students; he renounced everything and went to the mountains. He took just eight of his students, and he too disappeared into nothingness. I heard that Jesus did the same thing; for a while he went into solitude.

For us it's hard to give up even chocolate, but Shakyamuni gave up everything. And before he left his kingdom he would just give things away. His ministers were worried: it seemed that the contents of the treasury were disappearing fast! He didn't care. These things no longer mattered to him.

It's inspiring to look at the images of these holy beings as well as to read about them. I really like the statue of the skinny Buddha—the fasting Buddha, have you seen it? I think they have one in Afghanistan. It's so striking. It shows me so much about my own grasping mind. Look also at the more common statue of the Buddha, where he is shining, radiant. It signifies the clarity of Buddha's consciousness, his omnipresent wisdom.

These stories, these historical facts, these statues—they show us real human experience. They show us that what these yogis achieved, we can achieve. It is possible!

Many Kinds of Mahamudra

Both Paramitayana and Tantrayana explain universal reality, emptiness; it is the same nonduality that is being explained in both. In the text, Panchen Lama says,

> There are many ways to explain mahamudra, but they fall into two categories: sutra and tantra. . . .
> Sutra mahamudra is the way to meditate on empti-

ness taught explicitly in the extensive, intermediate, and condensed Perfection of Wisdom sutras.

Here, he gives the instructions according to the Perfection of Wisdom sutras and says that "The supreme arya, Nagarjuna, has stated that there is no path to liberation other than this."

Mahamudra can be described in many ways. For example, we Gelugpas sometimes say Middle Way, and the Nyingmapas talk about the Great Perfection, or *Dzogchen*. But they all refer to universal reality. The root text says,

> Although called by many names—innate union, the amulet box, the fivefold, equal taste, the four syllables, pacification, cutting off, great perfection, counsel on the middle-way view, and so on—when a yogi who is skilled in the scriptures and logic of definitive meaning and who has experience analyzes, all converge in a single intent.

There are differences, of course, philosophically and technically, but in principle they are the same. For example, according to some views we are already a buddha, but a Gelugpa might say, "How is that possible? If that's true, you don't need to meditate, receive teachings, and so on." You can argue like that, but it's just words. We need to taste the cake, that's all; arguing about the differences is a waste of time.

May Everyone Discover Mahamudra

Buddhism believes that any human being who has not discovered the universal reality of mahamudra is always suffering: being reborn again and again into the cycle of existence. Let's dedicate all our energy to all universal living beings who have not realized mahamudra: may they discover mahamudra.

3

The Preliminary Practices

The Gradual Path to Enlightenment

The beauty of the Buddhadharma is the way it is presented step by step. Drawing on his own experience, Shakyamuni Buddha presented his teachings in terms of stages. Lama Tsongkhapa took all this and presented it as the gradual path to enlightenment—what in Tibetan we call *lamrim*, the progressive development of the mind. By understanding these stages, we can see how to progress from our limited concepts, our limited view, to a limitless, universal view. So far as I know, this approach is unique to Buddhism.

Buddhist practice isn't about changing your name or your color, or putting an artificial label on yourself. No. It's about your own inner development, your own internal transformation. The stages of the path are set out in such a clean, clear way: "These are the preliminary practices. This is the main part. This is the result." It's intellectually comprehensible; you know what to do. In Buddhism, I feel, we haven't lost the key to enlightenment. We are so fortunate.

Homage to the Lama

Traditionally we present several preliminary practices before teaching mahamudra. I cannot avoid these; I have to explain them. Right at the beginning of the text, Panchen Lama pays homage to the guru:

> *Namo mahamudraya.* Homage to mahamudra, the
> all-pervasive nature of everything!

> I bow with respect at the feet of the incomparable
> guru,
> the lord of siddhas who teaches the naked [state of
> reality],
> the indivisible and inexpressible sphere of the vajra
> mind.

Next come the preliminary practices:

> First, earnestly go for refuge and generate bodhi-
> chitta. Since these are the gateway and the central
> pillar of the teachings and especially the Mahayana,
> this should not be mere words.

Refuge: Changing Our Attitude

The first practice is taking refuge in Buddha, Dharma, and Sangha. I'm sure you understand this already, but it is important to hear it again. When we take refuge, we change our attitude; we go beyond our normal attitude, which is to grasp at momentary, transitory pleasures. Those are what we usually take refuge in, aren't they? If we feel down, we go to the beach, jump in the water, and try to be a fish.

Or we turn to chocolate. But then we are dissatisfied because we ate too much—we tried to get satisfaction, but all we got instead was a fat belly! In the East we don't mind being fat, but in the West it's a big deal, isn't it?

So, practically speaking, taking refuge in Buddha, Dharma, and Sangha means we change our attitude. We see short-lived pleasures as unimportant, not worthwhile. We eliminate the ambitious, driving force of the grasping mind. That is what refuge means. It is vital we understand this.

Bodhichitta: Opening Up to Others

Next we can talk about actualizing *bodhichitta*, a Sanskrit word that can be translated as "enlightened attitude." With bodhichitta, your aim, your destination, is enlightenment. With it, you are totally open to other people, and not just superficially. You see others completely—their ultimate potential as well as their relative reality.

Sometimes you Westerners have an emotional idea about bodhichitta. "Oooh, bodhichitta, bodhichitta! All these suffering people! I must get all mother sentient beings to enlightenment!" Well, that's wrong. With bodhichitta you are relaxed, not upset. Sometimes you are so serious. You feel such urgency to help living beings, but you become too emotional. Bodhichitta is not like that. With bodhichitta you are easygoing, and there is much wisdom. You open your heart to all living beings and live that way as much as you can.

We have to establish this as our motivation. As Atisha said, the doorway to meditation, the starting point, is observing our attitude, our thought patterns, our motivation. Atisha was very practical.

You might say that living with bodhichitta is like having an experience of enlightenment itself; that is the connotation. When you open up hugely to others, your consciousness expands, becomes universal, almost omnipresent. This is extremely powerful. It's the same with an experience of nonduality. It's the feeling of omnipresent wisdom embracing all universal reality; there's no thought of *my* nonduality. These experiences are completely nonconceptual.

Combining the view of universal reality with the destination of enlightenment, bodhichitta, makes you psychologically easygoing, and small things don't bother you. What I mean is, sometimes we make small things big. Who cares if some big old tree out in the bush falls down! If the flower here on my table dies, it's okay. Or, speaking relatively, something "right" in Australia may be considered "wrong" in Singapore. This view of right and wrong has very little value. When you have a broad view, such small things are unimportant.

So, bodhichitta is very important. Don't think of it as some kind of religious attitude. No. It's completely scientific. It grows out of insight into reality, inner reality. It's unavoidable.

Vajrasattva: Destroying Negativity

The next preliminary practice is reciting the hundred-syllable mantra of Vajrasattva. The text says:

> Because seeing the reality of mind depends on amassing the collections and purifying negativity, first recite the hundred-syllable mantra . . .

In Tibetan Buddhism this practice is considered very important, so much so that all the traditions practice it— Nyingmapas, Kagyupas, and Sakyapas as well as us Gelugpas.

Vajrasattva is an emanation of Vajradhara, who is Shakyamuni Buddha in his tantric form. Vajrasattva is a manifestation of all the buddhas, but he represents in particular the energy of total purity. Visualizing ourselves as Vajrasattva is a powerful practice for destroying the dualistic view as well as the negativities that come from this dualistic mind. We need this kind of practice.

Since the ocean of our consciousness contains so many different kinds of negativity, we need various sophisticated ways to eliminate these problems; this is the function of the preliminary practices. Vajrasattva practice is considered the most powerful antidote of all—it can even purify broken root tantric vows.

There's No Negativity That Can't Be Purified

In the teachings you sometimes hear that there are certain vows that, if broken, that's it, there's no way out, no purification is possible. Of course, this is not actually true: there's no negativity that can't be purified. But sometimes it's good for our minds to hear it like this. The trouble is, Westerners take things so seriously! You're not flexible. "Oh, I broke my vows! I'm so scared! There's no way out! I have to go to hell!"

You see, Buddhism explains very clearly that this "no way out" relates to an individual situation. If I were to go into the ocean, I tell you, there *is* no way out! I will sink—unless you people quickly come and save me. It's true, I don't know how to swim, but that doesn't mean I don't have the potential to learn, does it? Tomorrow you can teach me how to swim; it's a dependent situation.

The Buddhist attitude is that it doesn't matter how many delusions you have, how confused you are, how much sin or negativity you have created, it is possible, absolutely possible, to totally eradicate all of it.

Negativity is like a cloud. When the sky is full of clouds and it's raining heavily, sometimes you feel that that's all there is. Well, sometimes it's the same for us psychologically, isn't it? But when the morning sun shines, the clouds are burned away, aren't they? Purification works in the same way: by applying the opposing energy, the negativity is cleared away. You purify the negative by actualizing the positive.

Negativity is a relative phenomenon; it is transitory, impermanent—in other words, it can be removed. You must recognize this. When you apply the opposing power of wisdom, there is no space for negativity; it's eliminated, burned up. That's how purification works.

It is vitally important that you realize that no matter how heavy the negative energy you've created, it can be eliminated. If you do not see this, your Dharma practice will be weak. After all, what Dharma practice *is* is eradicating all your negative energy. That is its purpose. We must recognize this.

For example, in the Western world we consider Hitler as the most sinful because he killed an unbelievable number of human beings. (I'm talking common sense here, not making a political point.) But from the Buddhist point of view Hitler can become enlightened too. Perhaps he has purified all that negativity and is enlightened already. It's possible!

Probably most of us here haven't killed any human beings—maybe we've killed a few mosquitoes, or fish, or other creatures. But look at Milarepa—he used black magic to kill at least thirty-five people, his mother's enemies. He wanted to show the power of his mother's son. But then he turned to the Dharma and achieved enlightenment in that very lifetime. For me, this is very encouraging. Milarepa is super! He had a super samsara and a super liberation.

Human beings are capable of anything. We can do *anything*. On the negative side, one human being is capable of destroying the entire solar system. And on the positive side, it is possible for one human being to lead all universal living beings to enlightenment. Human beings are more precious than any material thing.

Guru Yoga: Identifying with the Enlightened One

The fourth preliminary practice is called *guru yoga*. We consider this, too, to be especially important. At the moment, we are incapable of dealing with our ego, so Shakyamuni Buddha shows us how to handle it, how to eliminate the egotistic mind by identifying ourselves as the enlightened one.

In Mahayana Buddhism we believe that all living beings can achieve the realization of totality, of completeness, enlightenment: buddhahood. When we have reached that reality, there is no contradictory nature, there is no duality. There is only oneness: one universal understanding.

In guru yoga, we practice this by unifying our own consciousness with that of Guru Shakyamuni: our guru's consciousness and the Buddha's consciousness as one. The Tibetan term for yoga is *naljor*, and *jor* means "making close." In other words, guru yoga is becoming closer to our guru in the form of a buddha; we and the guru buddha become one. We shouldn't think, "My guru is higher, Shakyamuni is higher, and I'm the self-pity one. I'm impossible." We should not think this way.

In the Tibetan context *guru* has two meanings. There is the *relative* guru, the one who communicates with us in the world, who shows us how to act and how to find our own totality. And then there is the *inner* guru, the true meaning of *guru*: our own wisdom, our own clarity.

The relative guru, practically speaking, can do very little for the student. We see, for example, how a group of students all receiving the same teaching, the same instruction, can come to completely different understandings. Some reach the threshold of the teaching, some reach the center, some reach even further.

But our inner guru, our wisdom, can do the most powerful things. If we practice guru yoga, we learn to listen to our inner guru. Normally we listen only to our garbage talk; we don't listen to our wisdom. Even when wisdom does arise in our mind, we reject it.

These four—refuge, bodhichitta, the purification practice of Vajrasattva, and guru yoga—are the preliminary teachings of mahamudra. Older students have already had this kind of teaching, so I'm not going to elaborate on it so much here. But I did want to give you some framework for how the Tibetan tradition works. If you want to know more, and you have the time and space, do some research. In today's world, we have to go quickly on the path to enlightenment!

You Are the Cause of Your Enlightenment

During this meditation course I don't want you to think, "Lama Thubten Yeshe is going to make me enlightened." I don't want you to have that attitude. No, it's *you* who become a buddha, okay?

We are fortunate to be here, to share the teachings and our own understanding with each other. Here in this atmosphere, make a strong determination: "I want to become enlightened. I want to discover mahamudra." This attitude makes whatever place you are in conducive for meditation.

Energize one another as much as possible to achieve the realization of the universal reality of nonduality. Remember, this is the retreat approach, not some intellectual exercise. Then your meditation will become fruitful.

Again, fruitful results come not from me but from you. I pay respect to *your* buddha qualities.

PART 2

Practicing Mahamudra

4

First, Bring Your Mind to a Neutral State

The Position of the Body in Meditation

In order to achieve the realization of mahamudra, we first need to develop the subtle state of one-pointed concentration known as calm abiding—*shamata* in Sanskrit. But before we start to practice this technique, we need to neutralize our mind by doing the nine-round breathing meditation. Panchen Lama says,

> On a seat suitable for absorption, adopting the seven crucial points of physical posture, cleanse [the channels] with the nine-round breathing.

Lama Tsongkhapa recommends that you sit on a comfortable seat with your body slightly raised at the back. Cross your legs into the full-lotus position, with your right foot on the left thigh and your left foot on the right thigh. It might be difficult for beginners, so just come as close to it as you can.

Actually, if you can't sit cross-legged, that's okay. The most important thing is that your body is upright. Your head should be bent slightly forward. Your eyes should be half closed, without focusing on anything and looking toward the tip of your nose. However, if your mind is very distracted and you cannot quiet it, you might find it helpful to close your eyes.

Place the tip of your tongue against your palate just behind your front teeth, with your lower jaw relaxed. Your shoulders should be held back straight, not hunched forward. Your hands should be placed below your navel, resting in your lap, in the *mudra* of concentration, with the right one on top of the left and with your thumbs touching to form a triangle.

It is especially important to keep your mind and your body a little tight rather than loose; you can judge from your own experience. You need to train in this. Your body should be upright and slightly tight from the hips to the chest. Most of us slump, and a slumped posture can produce sluggishness. You can recognize yogis and yoginis by the way they hold their bodies.

I notice when some people meditate their body seems tense; they hold everything too tightly. That is not good, because the subtler wind energies in our body cannot flow properly. When you sit, try to be natural, relaxed, not tense.

Nine-Round Breathing Meditation

Nine-round breathing is an essential part of meditation practice. To comprehend universal reality, the mind needs to be in a neutral state. As we say in Tibet, a piece of white cloth can be transformed into any color. It's similar here: in order to transform your mind, you need to first neutralize it.

This is not merely visualization. As soon as you begin to practice it, you will feel some change. I always recommend this meditation before other meditations, including mahamudra. Calming down is the first step, and this nine-round breathing technique is a simple way to do that. You watch the movement of your breath and then gradually you become aware of your concepts.

Breathe out desire energy. Holding your left nostril closed with the back of your right index finger, breathe in slowly through your right nostril. Then block your right nostril with the front of the same finger and exhale through your left nostril. Think that you are breathing out all your impure desire energy. Do this three times. Actually, you don't need to hold the nostril closed; you can just visualize the air leaving through the other nostril.

Breathe out anger energy. Now do the reverse, using your left index finger: breathe in three times through the left nostril and, as you exhale through your right nostril, think that you are breathing out all your impure anger energy.

Breathe out ignorance energy. Finally, breathe in and out three times through both nostrils to make all the energies clean-clear and equal. As you exhale, think that you are breathing out all your impure ignorance energy. In total this makes nine rounds.

Breathe in pure energy. Whenever you breathe in, you can think you are inhaling pure blissful energy from all the lineage lamas, all the buddhas and bodhisattvas of the ten directions. When you exhale, think that all your physical and mental difficulties, the symptoms of your blocked energy, disappear.

Lama Tsongkhapa emphasizes that you should breathe in and out only through your nostrils, not through your mouth. Breathe in slowly and gently. When exhaling, first breathe out gently, then strongly, and then gently again.

Meditate on Guru Shakyamuni Buddha

Next, Panchen Lama says to "meditate on the profound path of guru yoga." You visualize Shakyamuni Buddha—as oneness with your guru, remember—and recite the mantra of Shakyamuni a few times: *Tadyatha om muni muni mahamuniye svaha.*

Often you think you can't visualize. It's true, visualizing Buddha is not your habit. But you *do* visualize all the time—usually your boyfriend or girlfriend! Delusions repeatedly create images, like photos in the mind.

Visualize Guru Shakyamuni Buddha in the space in front of you. He can be big or small—whatever is comfortable. Don't think of him as physical; his omnipresent wisdom manifests as a radiant golden light-body.

Now visualize at the center of your chest, where your heart chakra is, a yellow flame surrounded by the letters of the mantra, which are vibrating with reddish-yellow electric energy. Light radiates from the letters, automatically purifying all your impure concepts, while you recite the mantra a few times.

By the way, don't think this practice is some kind of Tibetan ritual; it is something very simple. When you say *muni muni mahamuniye*—"Conqueror, Conqueror, Great Conqueror"—think that you are conquering the egotistic mind. Saying *svaha* puts the realization of this into your heart.

> *Tadyatha om muni muni mahamuniye svaha, Tadyatha om muni muni mahamuniye svaha, Tadyatha om muni muni mahamuniye svaha.*

Purify the body. Next, imagine bright white laser beams shooting out of Guru Shakyamuni Buddha's brow chakra and entering into your brow chakra, filling your brain and your entire body, burning up all the heaviness of your body, transforming it into a radiant light-body.

Again, recite a few times as you visualize.

> *Tadyatha om muni muni mahamuniye svaha, Tadyatha om muni muni mahamuniye svaha, Tadyatha om muni muni mahamuniye svaha.*

Purify the speech. Next, Guru Shakyamuni Buddha sends from his throat chakra radiant red laser beams, which shoot into your throat chakra, burning up all your impure speech: the lies you tell, the harsh speech, and all the nonsense, all the blah, blah, blah—throughout our life, our speech is almost endless nonsense. All this is burned up, and your throat chakra fills up with the blissful radiant red light energy.

Tadyatha om muni muni mahamuniye svaha, Tadyatha om muni muni mahamuniye svaha, Tadyatha om muni muni mahamuniye svaha.

Purify the mind. Now Guru Shakyamuni Buddha sends from his heart chakra blissful radiant blue light, which sinks into your heart, destroying all your dualistic, fanatical thinking, all the negative mental energy. Your heart chakra is filled with blissful, radiant blue light energy.

Tadyatha om muni muni mahamuniye svaha, Tadyatha om muni muni mahamuniye svaha, Tadyatha om muni muni mahamuniye svaha.

Dissolve the guru into yourself. Finally, imagine that Guru Shakyamuni Buddha becomes small, comes to sit above your crown facing the same way as you, and then sinks into your central channel and down to your heart chakra. As the Panchen Lama says:

After making hundreds of fervent requests and so on, dissolve the guru into yourself.

Imagine that Guru Buddha's consciousness and your consciousness unify, becoming one. Contemplate this experience. Let go, let go . . .

If dualistic concepts come up, repeat the experience. Let the Buddha again sink into your heart, and again contemplate your mind, the guru's mind, and Buddha's mind becoming one.

We Must Practice

Now that you've experienced some meditation, you need to practice. This life is very short, and we are fortunate to have it, so determine that you will do your best to discover reality, touch reality.

And you must participate with others, and try to be a good example. Participation is like compassion. Even if you are enlightened, you simply interact with mother sentient beings. Shakyamuni Buddha came to this earth as an ordinary man; out of his universal compassion, his great compassion, he came, he lived. This is compassion, Buddha's way. He had already totally gone beyond ego, beyond sensory-gravitation attachment, so he did not need to engage with others for his own benefit. His participation on this earth was only because of his great compassion, to help others.

The self-cherishing thought is, "*I* am suffering. *I* miss my boyfriend. *I* miss my girlfriend. *I* am missing chocolate." Simply watching the way you behave with others is compassion.

5

The Benefits of Samadhi Are Incredible

Without Calm Abiding We Cannot Realize Mahamudra

As I mentioned, to achieve the realization of mahamudra, the reality of nonduality, we first need to develop calm abiding. In fact, it is not possible without it. We must achieve the subtler levels of consciousness of indestructible one-pointed concentration, what in Sanskrit we call *samadhi*.

It is difficult to realize nonduality *not* because it's hiding from us but because our concepts are so thick. So we must refine, *refine* our concepts; we must achieve subtle mindfulness, subtle awareness, and subtle clarity. Otherwise, there is no way we can see the unconscious levels of ego grasping an independent self. Not possible!

Samadhi is the source of liberation. Without perfect samadhi, then, there is no *way* to become liberated from samsara and no *way* to achieve enlightenment. There is no exception: whether we are Christian, Muslim, Hindu, or Buddhist, to cut the dualistic view we need calm abiding.

But Calm Abiding Is Not Enough

On the other hand, some people actually think that this state of samadhi, this one-pointed concentration, is all we need in order to cut ego. But that is wrong. Lama Tsongkhapa reminds us that calm abiding alone is not enough to cut the dualistic view. We also need to develop special insight, or *vipashyana* in Sanskrit. In Tibetan we call it *lhagtong*—*lhag* meaning "extra" and *tong* meaning "seeing." We can interpret this to mean that we go beyond seeing conventional reality and achieve the "extra seeing" of the universal reality of mahamudra.

In other words, we need the two kinds of meditation together: calm abiding and special insight.

The Benefits of Samadhi Are Incredible

Nevertheless, even without special insight, the results of samadhi alone are unbelievable, almost unimaginable. When we understand this, when we realize how amazing the results are, we cannot help but try to develop it. There is no way we become lazy; we will have much energy and make great effort. We won't even worry about eating.

I will explain some of the benefits.

You Go Beyond Sensory and Conceptual Consciousness

As your concentration develops, you will go beyond your body. Your mind will be nonconceptual, so it becomes *easy* to cut the complex world of the five sense objects, to eliminate the superstitions. In such a unified state, your mind becomes so subtle, so sharp, you can easily eradicate the complex dualistic thoughts. You can touch reality. This is the *feature* of samadhi.

And out of meditation you can *easily* deal with your delusions; they are so light, you can stop them immediately.

You Experience Bliss

In the subtle state of concentration, you experience bliss—ecstatic bliss—just naturally. The more concentration you have, the more integrated you are, and thus the more rapture, the more bliss, you experience.

In the beginning, the bliss you experience is physical, which is the grosser level. But as your concentration deepens, as you throw off the layers of blankets of grosser consciousness, you experience bliss exclusively at the mental level. This is because you have stopped perceiving the objects of the five senses, you have closed the door to superstition. All the contradictory concepts have disappeared. Your mind is now crystal clear.

As If You Could Count Every Atom

As your concentration gets stronger and you reach ever-subtler levels, your mind becomes super powerful. From his own experience, Lama Je Tsongkhapa says that you can reach a point of such clarity in your meditation that your mind feels almost infinite.

Your mind is so clear, so sharp, it's as if you can distinguish all the subtle physical energies. You'll have the courageous thought, "I can count *all* the atoms of the universe!" This level of mind is more powerful than even scientific instruments. Now I think I'm showing pride in Buddhism!

You Will Have an Experience of Space

As you develop your concentration on the clarity of your consciousness, you will reach a point where you will be only at the conscious level, as we discussed. You have gone beyond the physical, beyond the world of the five senses. Because you have thrown off the blankets of the superstitions, the heavy wrong conceptions, you will feel so unified, and you will have an experience of space, universal space.

You Are Always Joyful

When you arise from your meditation you feel liberated instead of uncertain and full of doubts and conflicts. You experience inner peace; you will always have a happy, joyful vibration. In fact, you continuously experience tremendous pleasure—now the pleasure of chocolate is nothing to you!

What you can now experience with your mind is super. It's like another realm, another dimension. And when your senses do come into contact with their objects, of course, you experience bliss then too.

You hardly even notice whether it's night or day. Actually, even now, when you have samsaric happiness, you have a similar kind of experience. You dance and drink all night, intoxicated with the pleasure: time just flies. "Oh, now it's morning already?" Well, this is what happens when you're intoxicated with the blissful experience of samadhi. And, of course, this shows that time is not fixed from the outside; it's made up by the mind.

Your Body Feels So Light

When you are out of meditation, the heavy energy of your body vanishes. Your body feels like a brand new body. You feel so light, almost as if you could fly, almost as if you had no body at all. To some extent you can see this in your ordinary daily life. When your mind is satisfied, your body feels light, doesn't it?

Your Sleep Is Like Meditation

Lama Tsongkhapa says that because you have developed such clarity in your concentration meditation, even in your dreams your experience of the superstitions, your conceptions about the five sense objects, will be much lighter. Your sleep will be like meditation. Normally we experience heavy impure projections in our dreams, but when we have good concentration we can experience pure visions.

You Develop Clairvoyance

Lama Tsongkhapa says that you will develop clairvoyance. According to the Abhidharma teachings, there are two kinds of clairvoyance. One is what we understand as "intuition," an untrained sense that we all have to some extent. For example, you might feel strongly, without any logical proof, that something has happened to your dear friend back home.

The other can be gained by training the mind in meditation, as we are discussing here. You are able to see long distances, as well as other people, including their minds. At first, your experiences seem a bit like a dream, but the more your concentration develops, the more clearly you can see, just as you would if you were there in person. Maybe you can even touch far-away forms.

This kind of clairvoyance is not imagining something. It's real, in the present, not a fantasy. Normally, with your deluded thoughts, you create images of your boyfriend in your mind when he's not here, let's say, and it's almost as if he's real. But when it's clairvoyance, you literally see your boyfriend.

You May Get a Taste of Nonduality

At the subtler level of consciousness achieved in samadhi meditation, your wisdom will be so powerful, so sharp, just naturally. Automatically you will have some experience of nonduality, of mahamudra, of no subject and object—because in this unified state of samadhi, the complex dualistic thoughts have temporarily ceased.

We could intellectually debate this. "How can you stop the superstitions? It's not until you reach the tenth level of the bodhisattva stages that they have ceased. Yet here you are saying that if you reach certain levels of concentration you can achieve the experience of nonduality, non-superstition."

Well, you can debate like this, yes. But when you understand these subtler levels of consciousness, you will see the logic of this assertion. Here we are talking about experience. At a certain point you have to abandon these philosophical arguments. When I received the mahamudra teachings from my guru, he said exactly this. I remember it! At first I didn't understand; my misconceptions were so strong then.

You May Experience the Dissolutions

As a result of deep concentration it's possible to bring the deluded energies—the winds and the delusions themselves—into the central channel. This is similar to what happens at death. You feel as if you're disappearing; even the breath stops. Experiencing the various visions associated with the dissolution of the subtler energies is a sign of good concentration (as we will see in chapter 11).

If this happens, instead of being afraid, just let go; keep your awareness, your memory or mindfulness. At each stage in this dissolution process, the mind gets finer, subtler.

But if you become unconscious, that is not right.

You Can Gain These Realizations

Know that if you put effort into cultivating samadhi, you can gain these realizations. It's possible because of the simple power of habit. From the Buddhist point of view, every human being has the potential for clarity, for bliss, which eventually can lead to the experience of universal reality.

And, of course, the more you experience your own potential for clarity and bliss, the deeper your concentration becomes, and the happier you are to meditate. So, you must learn to turn on the switch of your own ecstatic blissful energy.

NO POSTAGE
NECESSARY
IF MAILED
IN THE
UNITED STATES

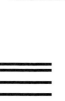

BUSINESS REPLY MAIL
FIRST-CLASS MAIL   PERMIT NO. 1100   SOMERVILLE, MA

POSTAGE WILL BE PAID BY ADDRESSEE

WISDOM PUBLICATIONS
199 ELM ST
SOMERVILLE MA 02144-9908

Wisdom

WISDOM PUBLICATIONS

Please fill out and return this card if you would like to receive our catalogue and special offers. The postage is already paid!

NAME

ADDRESS

CITY / STATE / ZIP / COUNTRY

EMAIL

Sign up for our newsletter and special offers at wisdompubs.org

Wisdom Publications is a non-profit charitable organization.

6

Before Meditating on Your Mind, Establish What It Is

The Conventional Nature of Our Mind

Normally we meditate on Buddha's image, on the breath, or on other things, but in mahamudra meditation we contemplate our own mind, our consciousness. So, what is the mind? What are its characteristics?

From the Buddhist point of view, consciousness has no substantial or physical characteristics. It has no color and no form. You could say it's like space. It has a clean-clear nature, clear-light nature. In Tibetan we call it *selshing rigpa*. *Sel* means "clear," *rigpa* means "to see," "to know." Exactly as Panchen Lama says, consciousness is "that which is clear and knowing." This clarity is its conventional, relative nature.

Consciousness perceives reality like a mirror does: it reflects. However, if a mirror is not clear—if it's dusty, let's say—it cannot reflect accurately, can it? An unclear mind cannot reflect reality accurately either.

Yet even our dualistic concepts, our deluded thoughts such as desire and hatred, possess this clarity. This is why they can, to some extent, perceive their projections; why they have the ability to reflect their own object: the desire object, the hatred object. A good example is water when it's boiling: it's turbulent, but still it possesses the same clear nature as water when it's still. It's the same for our dualistic concepts: they, too, are essentially clear in their nature.

The Ultimate Nature of Our Mind

As we discussed before, delusions can be totally eradicated. Maitreya uses the example of tarnished gold. The tarnish is not in the character of the gold, is it? So it can be removed. It's the same with the mind: negativities are there, but because they are not in the nature of the mind they can be removed.

Here I'm talking relatively. Ultimately, then, there's no discussion about whether the mind is pure or not: it is absolutely pure. The mind has no trace of ego-nature. Its nature *is* clear light, nonduality, non–self-existence. In other words, the essential nature of our mind, of thought, of consciousness, is purity.

I'm not saying you're enlightened already; I'm not saying that. This purity is our buddha potential. This fundamental, clear-light nature of our mind exists always within us. It's a matter of recognizing it.

The Mind and Its Objects

Fundamentally there are two things: our consciousness, which is the subject, and the world of sense objects—things, people, sounds, smells, and so on. Normally, we are distracted by the objects of our senses, aren't we? Most of the time the arising of our superstitions, our dualistic conceptions, is linked to the sensory objects, including sentient beings. According to Buddhism, our five senses have a bad reputation; they are the doorway to the superstitions, to the ego; they are set up to activate delusions. The moment we open our sense perceptions to the world, the reflections come, and then we conceptualize, categorize: this, that, this, that. This is the problem.

Say we're observing a person. Normally we are busy putting our projections onto them; we never observe our mind's *view* of the person, our thoughts about the person. As soon as the reflection of you comes into my mind and I start thinking you are this and that, my mind becomes disturbed, like a tornado. The reflection of you, the appearance of you, coming into my mind is not the problem. The problem is all my judgments about you. We need to throw out this habit!

Happiness and Suffering Come from Our Mind

From the Buddhist point of view, all the circumstances of samsara and nirvana are manifestations of our mind. This is the central understanding. All the suffering, the happiness, liberation, the highest realizations—all manifest from our consciousness.

Our day-to-day life is controlled by the mind. We can see this. When the wish to go to the beach arises, the thought of desire takes us to the beach. Maybe we're tired of Western society and want an easy life, no responsibilities, so we think, "Maybe I'll go to India." This thought takes us to India. Our grasping mind leads us wherever we go.

Or we change our opinions about things all the time. Let's say you're young and you get fed up with home and leave your country. You hate it! But then you go back years later, when your mind is more healthy, and now it's beautiful. Such contradictory experiences come from our mind, not the object—we know this. And this is the evidence of selflessness, isn't it?

This modern world is so complicated. Our daily life involves so much intellectualizing. We create all the thoughts of good, bad, black, white, the superstitions, all the artificial concepts. We build up all these dualistic concrete bricks. We overestimate everything, or we underestimate; we are so extreme, so unbalanced. The great yogi Shantideva said that our deluded mind is like a mad elephant, completely out of control. We need to control the mind, not have delusions control us.

As children our minds were more simple, more natural, and as we got older we acquired more and more concepts, more hallucinated projections, more fantasies; we repeat and repeat the good, bad, good, bad mantra. These are the hindrances that prevent us from touching our deepest human nature, from touching reality, our potential for eternal peace.

With mahamudra meditation, we can knock down these dualistic bricks and become more natural, more simple, more down to earth.

Meditating on the Mind Is Not Mahamudra, But It Leads to It

Using our own mind as the object of concentration is the unique characteristic of mahamudra meditation that makes it such a powerful method for eliminating our dualistic thinking. However, contemplating our own consciousness does not bring the actual realization of mahamudra—ultimate reality—because the mind is still relative reality. But it leads to it.

Using our own consciousness as the object of meditation leads to the experience of mahamudra because it brings an experience *similar* to mahamudra. Because mind is clean-clear in its nature, we can cut through the busyness of conceptuality, cut the gross dualistic thoughts, and begin to experience the clarity of our consciousness, its relative nature.

Eventually we unify the indestructible concentration gained in calm abiding meditation on this clarity with a subtle wisdom that analyzes the dualistic view, which leads to special insight, the realization of ultimate reality. This is the nucleus of the great yogi Lama Tsongkhapa's method for developing mahamudra.

In short, we start with concentrating on our own consciousness, and then we meditate on emptiness.

7

Now, Meditate on
Your Mind

Maybe you're not sure what it means to "meditate on your mind." Actually, it's simple. The mahamudra way is to start by contemplating your concepts, the views of your own thoughts. Eventually this leads to experiencing the clarity of your consciousness, its conventional nature.

We observe the thoughts, and then we let go. *No* intellect— we don't analyze our thoughts. Leaving the mind as it is like this is the special emphasis of this meditation. In our gradual-path meditations we analyze. But mahamudra meditation emphasizes *not* analyzing. Because when the mind is analyzing, it's trembling, shaking. It's like an airplane when it's turning; it shakes, doesn't it?

Lama Tsongkhapa says that when we contemplate the consciousness, we should not follow any object, such as form or color or sound, or even the image of a buddha, a mantra, or a syllable. These we should abandon.

We refer to this approach as "nonconceptual," "nonsuperstitious." In Tibetan we say, *mitogpa kyongwa*: "maintaining a nonconceptual state of mind." I think this is very sensible, very logical. Of course, our habit to follow the five sense objects is strong, so we need to learn to develop the skill in meditation to stay on the consciousness itself.

As I mentioned, for Lama Tsongkhapa, using our own mind as the object of concentration in mahamudra meditation is a very sensitive, direct method. It *easily* eliminates the superstitions and confusion—this is the *point*—and therefore *easily* leads to the realization of the universal reality of nonduality, emptiness.

The Two Main Obstacles in Meditation

Countless obstacles prevent us from obtaining perfect concentration, but we can include them in two categories: one is distractedness and the other is sluggishness.

Distractedness. Our mind becomes distracted, or wanders, because we're overwhelmed by our usual delusions: desire, anger, and the rest. And, of course, it also wanders because of laziness. We don't make enough effort to concentrate because we don't yet have enough understanding of the incredible benefits of concentration, like those discussed above. We understand really well the benefits of going to the supermarket—all that supermarket goodness! We understand the results of our samsaric activities, but they are nothing compared to experiencing our own clarity.

Gross sluggishness. Sluggishness has both gross and subtle levels. Gross sluggishness, when our mind is cloudy or we feel like falling asleep, is more easily recognizable. There is a skillful way to stop it. As we are contemplating the clarity of our thoughts, we might have a slight impression of darkness: this is one sign of sluggishness. It's like when we're sitting outside on a sunny day and a light cloud moves across the sun. So in our meditation, the moment we get an impression of darkness, we need to adjust our object of meditation, making it a little clearer, a little stronger. We learn to develop the skill to know how to do this.

In your effort to make the object clear, clear, clear, however, you risk applying so much effort that you become totally distracted. It is possible to go too far. So be careful.

Subtle sluggishness. When we reach a certain stage of very deep concentration, the major obstacle is subtle sluggishness, but it is very difficult to recognize. We can easily mistake subtle sluggishness for correct concentration. We can stay there, effortlessly, forever. That's dangerous. Some meditators think they have perfect concentration; there is no wandering, no superstition, no sensory feelings, only a very blissful experience. They feel, "This is fantastic! Someone could cut me with a knife and I wouldn't feel pain. Now I no longer have any sensory attachment."

Yes, the mind has indeed become subtler, but it is not fully mindful; there is no intensive wisdom. It's like sleeping. This is subtle sluggishness. Maybe for most of us it will be a long time before we need to worry about this danger!

No Need to Clean the Mind

Now let's practice. Just watch your thoughts. Maybe not *literally* watch—language is a problem. Be like the sunlight, which merely shines.

Normally we think our mind is bad, deluded, and that we have to make it clean. But mind's nature is clean-clear: clarity is a fundamental characteristic of mind. In Buddhism, this applies both in philosophy and in meditation. You don't need to make effort to make your mind this way or that; you just need to leave it alone. Its clear-light nature is pure from the beginning, and this nature exists forever.

If you can find the object to some extent, then just let go, let go. If you try too hard to make it bright, you will lose it, and distraction will come.

No Expectations

Abandon expectations, any hope, say, for a high realization. Abandon expectations of any kind, in fact. Just let go. Keep the concentration strong and be satisfied with that.

Losang Chokyi Gyaltsen says you should not "allow your conceptual mind to entertain any fears or expectations and enter equipoise without the slightest distraction."

In other words, when you've reached a reasonably clean-clear point, without emotional disturbance, don't start worrying or get too excited. No! Just leave it there.

Avoid Even Positive Concepts

Avoid all concepts, even positive ones such as, "How wonderful if all sentient beings can reach buddhahood!" That is not valid here. Even if you have a memory of your past life as some Himalayan yogi or you have some fantastic vision—even if the Buddha comes!—do not follow it. Let go of it immediately.

Don't think that I'm trying to get you to forget about everything, your normal life. "Maybe I should just go to sleep and forget everything." No! Panchen Lama mentions this: "It's not the cessation of mental activity as when you faint or fall asleep." In the development of concentration, all such thoughts are interferences. That is why you need to stop following them.

Because our habit to go to the form, the sound, the color, the smell, is so deep, we must use great skill to keep your awareness strongly on your consciousness. Keep mindfulness, or memory, continuously. Panchen Lama says:

> Begin keeping watch with undistracted mindfulness and, with alertness, make your mind attentive to any movement.

We also have the habit to go to the past or the future; we get so distracted. We must break this habit, too. Remain focused on the clean-clear state of our own consciousness. The yogi Tilopa says to place the mind on the consciousness alone, without anything else. Eventually our muddy consciousness, our superstitions, will settle and become clear. Continuous nonstop mindfulness is the resource of awareness.

Like the Sun

Your consciousness is like the sun. Just like the sun's rays shoot out from the sun, your thoughts, your views—right views and wrong views—manifest from your consciousness. Whatever thought you experience, keep your mindfulness of it continuously. That is the meditation.

Like Space

Your mind is like space. When the rain comes, the space is not disturbed. Rain falls, but still it's part of space. When the rain is strong, it's disturbing, but when it stops, things become quiet and peaceful again.

The rainfall is similar to your superstitions: when they are manifesting, it's disturbing, but they still have nonduality nature, still the original nature.

Like the Ocean

Your mind is like the blue ocean. It's there, you just watch it. Your thoughts are like the waves. Waves manifest from the ocean, but they are still part of the ocean. When a wave rises out of the ocean, there's some turbulence. When it drops back into the ocean again, it's not different from the ocean, is it?

Like the Full Moon

Your consciousness is like the full moon. On this earth all the people and fishes and chickens and trees—all the organic things—are moving, functioning. But the full moon is just there.

Your intensive awareness remains intensive awareness of consciousness, even though the distractions themselves are coming and going. They no longer energize you. They no longer distract you. You remain on your mind with intensive mindfulness.

As Losang Chokyi Gyaltsen says, "Tighten by making taut and look nakedly at the nature of that which is clear and knowing"—your mind, in other words—and "recognize any conceptual thoughts that arise."

Learn to Let Go

When you reach the point where you can experience the clarity of your consciousness, then try to let go. Keep your concentration a little loose rather than exerting tremendous effort. Don't squeeze your mind. Too much effort, too strict discipline, is not good. You need to learn to let go.

Keep your mindfulness continuous and experience the clarity. When the mind is stable, let go. In this state, you experience quiet, joyfulness, even bliss.

"Let go" has many meanings. When you drive a car, for example, once you're aware of the right speed, the overall situation, then you need to just let go, relax. When you relax you can enjoy the drive. It's almost as if the car is flying, isn't it?

But new drivers can't do that. They're always trying to adjust things; they're too nervous, too tense.

It's the same with new meditators. You have to learn to let go. If you don't know how to let go, you can never experience bliss. When you try too hard, you get headaches and high blood pressure, and eventually you hate meditation. Just the sight of your meditation cushion makes you want to go nowhere near it! So learning to let go is extremely important.

When you know how to let go, the root text says, you will be liberated from superstition. "When mind bound in a tangle is relaxed, without doubt it frees itself." When you know how to let go, you taste the blissful chocolate cake of meditation. Then each time you go to meditate, you will enjoy it.

Don't Reject Distractions

Don't feel bad when distractions come. Don't get upset and reject them. There's no need to think, "Oh, this is ego. It is bad." Recognize that these deluded thoughts, the dualistic thoughts, the superstitions, are simply a manifestation of your consciousness. Look at the essential nature of the thoughts: they are also clear in their nature, as we discussed. When they come, instead of rejecting them, look, then penetrate into their essential nature.

Or think that the thoughts are like the birds, the airplanes, all the organic things that move in the space of your consciousness; they come and they go. Just let go. You can use your awareness to watch the essence of the superstitions; you don't need to lose the awareness. Panchen Lama says that you should

> recognize as movement [of the mind] whatever conceptual thoughts are generated and, without blocking them, focus on their nature.

If Too Distracted, Relax and Watch the Breath

If the distractions are too strong, it's better to stop the meditation on the consciousness and do the nine-round breathing meditation. Or you can simply watch the breath. Breathing meditation is simple. Breathe, but don't think about the breathing. Using the breathing techniques, we can help our super-sensitive schizophrenic mind calm down so that we can again contemplate the clear mirror of our own consciousness.

Sometimes people don't know how to breathe, and that creates tension. Notice that when you are sad or depressed, you sigh deeply, don't you? Breathing is very important for health. You should be sensitive to the movement of your breath. Breathing well can even energize bliss, while breathing wrongly can cause problems.

These techniques can quickly cut the gross levels of the superstitions, and soon you'll reach a point where your mind is more neutral and you can go back to the clarity of your mind.

Persevere. And Be Satisfied

It's important to put energy into the practice from the beginning. And to not give up. The Vinaya texts illustrate this with an example: If you want to make fire by rubbing two sticks together, you have to be persistent. You can't just give up and then start over; it will never work. It's the same with your concentration.

Lama Tsongkhapa emphasizes that when you get some experience of clarity, be satisfied. Don't think, "Oh, this not enough clarity; this is not what my lama means." You understand? You're over-intellectualizing. You need to discover what is right through experience; don't go by mere words.

Perhaps you have special experiences in meditation, and then they go away. Don't be disappointed. They are valuable. They are *your* experiences. It has nothing to do with intellect, nothing to do with the books, nothing to do with my words. It's important to recollect these experiences. They show you what you can achieve. At other times you can have perfect experiences, but you don't recognize them. You just throw them into the garbage.

When I do retreat, I have some experiences too—small experiences. When I recollect my retreat, I am satisfied. I am not saying I have great experiences, but they're good enough. I think all of us can have moments of bliss—or even of simply not being disturbed by the concepts. That's super! Remember these times. They're *your* experiences, not anyone else's.

Retain the Clarity Outside of Meditation

With mahamudra you don't need to do anything formal. The clarity of your mind is with you twenty-four hours a day, so it's possible to retain the experience during your breaks as well. You use your mindfulness and leave your mind on the clarity of your own thoughts.

This is very simple. You can apply it in any situation: while you're drinking tea, while you're eating, walking, talking—even while you're dreaming. Part of your mind is always aware of the clarity of the thoughts.

Normally, you're busy with your fantasies, transfixed by your thoughts and ideas. Or you're always thinking, "Oh, I'm so confused," and there's no sense of clarity. But the clarity of your mind is always accessible. It makes no difference whether you are feeling confused or miserable, blissful or fantastically clear. All these feelings are your mind, and they are clear in their nature.

Every situation can become a meditation. Just watch your own mind, the views moving through your mind. When your emotions are strong, instead of focusing on the object, the person, focus on the mind itself. Sit back and observe the clean-clear nature of the feelings themselves. Instead of making your mind busy with the dualistic judgments about the person or other external things, simply keep your mindfulness on the subject, on mind itself.

At a certain point you will become clear. You keep your mindfulness on whatever's arising, and you let go, without intellectualizing or analyzing. Okay?

This is beautiful. Whatever situation you're in, you immediately remember the clarity. Once you've developed this habit, you can bring it into any situation. You're developing mindfulness. That's what concentration meditation *is*.

8

Before Meditating on Mahamudra, Establish What Exists and What Doesn't

We're Just a Name

The great second-century Indian scholar Nagarjuna describes the way we exist. The combination of our five aggregates—our form, feeling, discrimination, nonassociated compounded phenomena, and consciousness—is given a name. The name is a label, which comes from a concept. That is it. That is the reality, conventional reality. No more.

But the characteristic of ego-mind is that it's always dissatisfied with that reality. And this ego-mind—perhaps it's better that we say "ego-wisdom," because in a sense ego is so intelligent, so skillful—completely knocks out our reality.

We can also say we're a combination of the six elements—the usual four plus consciousness and space. To these elements a name is given. The name comes from the mind; the mind looks at this combination, then gives it a name, a label, and this is the conventional reality. It doesn't matter how important we hold it to be, the way it exists is no more than that. I mean it: *no more*!

The root text quotes Nagarjuna:

> The individual is not earth, is not water,
> is not fire, is not wind, is not space,
> is not awareness, it is not all of these.
> Yet, what individual is there other than these?

In other words, if we go looking for something more among each of the six elements, no way can we find anything there either. In Buddhist terminology, this is the meaning of *conventional*: in itself a phenomenon is not absolute. But the ego holds things as absolute. Ego *wants* absolute me. We hold on to an absolute I, which is totally nonexistent. There is no absolute I; nor are there absolute six elements, absolute five aggregates. There are none, scientifically.

When we understand this we see that if something *were* existing from itself, it couldn't change. Nothing exists like that!

Ego Exaggerates

Ego wants, ego *wants*. When it's summertime and it's a hundred degrees, the ego wants absolute-reality Coca-Cola. Coca-Cola becomes the absolute solution. This view is totally wrong; it's exaggeration. Coca-Cola does have a relative, conventional, artificial quality, but how can we say it is absolute?

When the ego-mind cognizes something, there is no room to accept it *as it is*; ego-mind has to go beyond the relative way that the thing exists. For this reason, Buddhism emphasizes understanding interdependence as the logic to prove nonduality, non–self-existence. We already understand this to some extent.

There Is No Scott

Take Scott, for example. We give the name "Scott" to the group of six elements sitting here. There is this combination here, and then we say the name "Scott." Three things are involved in this process: your mind, the name, and the conventional reality of Scott's six elements. Okay, there must be some reason we say "Scott"; there *is* some reason, always there is some reason. But that reason is superficial; there is no absolute quality at all.

There is *no* absolute phenomenon there. Something just occurred, like some wind coming . . . Scott is coming. All there is, what Scott is, is just some interdependent phenomenon linked with the thought: our superstitious, conceptual thought says the word "Scott." All this is just a bubble; *so* interdependent.

There is this combination, these parts, and then we give a name to them, that's all. We cannot go *further* than that. We cannot say, "Scott is special." But we are looking for more than that, something objectively existing; our ego is not satisfied—

especially if we are attracted to Scott and we project a quality of handsomeness onto him.

Our ego tries to project handsomeness onto him almost beyond his capacity. When we go beyond the interdependent, conventional level, then it becomes absolute. But it's a false absolute, isn't it? Maybe today we can hold that projection, but tomorrow it disappears.

And then from *his* side, his own ego's side, he also doesn't want to accept himself at the conventional, superficial level, as an interdependent phenomenon. His ego also goes beyond the conventional reality of himself. His ego is also holding such a concept of "handsome," which is absolute for him. He puts that label onto parts of himself: sometimes he puts it on his eyes, sometimes on his nose, sometimes his mouth, sometimes his neck—perhaps his navel chakra! He tries, he tries, but *no way*. It's like he's forcing extra things onto himself.

In other words, what I am saying is that he holds such an absolute, *un*changeable, *un*conventional, *un*superficial view. He feels, "This is my reality."

Scott Is Merely Labeled

Scott does not exist in *any* of the elements of his body, *any* of the parts of his mind. It's like a car before it's assembled in the factory: it's just a bunch of things, right? It's not a car then. That combination of parts is not the car. It's the same with Scott: the combination of Scott's parts is not him.

Now, if we put Scott in front of a mirror, there are two things, right? The reflection of Scott in the mirror and Scott in front of it. So, in our judgment, we think, "Scott is the true one; the one in the mirror is just a reflection, it's not Scott."

But from the point of view of the great yogis Nagarjuna and Lama Tsongkhapa, within both of these spheres—the body of Scott and the reflection of Scott—there is no Scott existing. The reflection is not him, and neither is the bubble of his elements. Both equally are not him. It's not, "Ah, the combination of parts is Scott and the reflection is not." Normally we think this. But realistically, if you try to find Scott within these two spheres, you cannot. No way.

Scott comes from the name, the label. *That* is why he is existing. Other people's concepts produce the artificial name, the label; then Scott exists. For this reason, all conventional reality is produced by the superstitious mind. For this reason, Scott is not earth, Scott is not water, Scott is not fire, Scott is not consciousness, Scott is not space.

Between the elements and the name, the superficial view, that is the only existing Scott. We cannot go further. All there is is the totality of Scott, the nonexistence of Scott, the mahamudra of Scott. But we want to go beyond the name, don't we?

The conclusion is: Each of the elements individually is not Scott. And the group of them, the combination, is not Scott. Becoming Scott *depends* on the label, the name, being given to the elements. This connection between the name and the elements is the way that Scott exists. The operation of these is Scott.

When we nonconceptualize in meditation our experience of Scott, our mind reaches beyond the conventions of Scott. If we stay there awhile, contemplating, and then after our session we open up to his atmosphere, his elements, he'll seem like a mirage: Is he there or not there? Is he real or not real?

Somehow there is some vibration there, but it's not absolute. In other words, the absolute Scott disappears. When we are seeing with the ego, we always feel that Scott is absolute, which is totally wrong; it's because we have not tasted the nonduality of Scott.

We Really Believe "I'm Here"

Here we talk about Scott; I use him as an example. But it's the same for each of us. We feel, "I'm so solid. I am this, I am that." We believe, "I'm the important one."

We hold a dualistic view of our own self. Our responsibility is to observe this view, the way ego-mind grasps the I as self-existent. Do I exist as I believe, or not? We have to check that out.

We really feel that somewhere within our body or mind "I'm here." This is a totally wrong conception! It means that we do not recognize how things operate conventionally, how they exist interdependently. We can't accept it. We feel that we have some absolute reality.

The Conventional Self Exists Only for the Relative Mind

During mahamudra meditation we are not trying to destroy the conventional view of I—anyway, this is not the problem. The great yogi, the enlightened one Tilopa, said to his disciple Naropa, "My son, you are not bound by awareness itself.

You are kept in bondage by your concepts; they have such a tight hold."

In other words, the reflection of phenomena appearing in my mind is not itself the problem. The problem is that we stimulate the mind, shake the mind with the dualistic opinions: you are this, you are that. So we need to learn to not judge with such artificial concepts: this is good, that is bad. You understand? We need to eliminate this kind of thinking and to broaden our view of reality.

I want you to understand that the conventional I exists *only* for the conventional mind, a valid conventional mind. But ego-mind feels that there is an I here that isn't dependent, that exists without depending on any other phenomenon, that is solid. *That* is ego's concept.

Conventional, relative Coca-Cola operates only for the relative mind. It is not possible for Coca-Cola to become absolute. It is a combination of elements gathered together, then we give it a name, then it becomes Coca-Cola. It's the same with ourselves: what we call "I am this, I am that" is only the connection between the name and the elements. That's the only way we exist.

Because of our superstitions, our delusions, we create the fantasy of conventional existence. But the ego-mind doesn't want to accept this; it wants to make it absolute. But it's not possible.

We Need to Knock Out the Intuitive Ego

The problem is: as long as we hold the concept that our self exists objectively within the five aggregates, that such an I is existing from itself, without depending on anything, then we do not touch reality—we either overestimate or underestimate. So the unique skill of this mahamudra meditation technique is that it banishes these conceptions.

Seeing things as absolute in this way, holding the concept of an independent I, is not an intellectually created idea of ego, philosophically made up. We could supplement one philosophical view about ego for another, but this will not solve our problem. We need to knock out the *intuitive* ego, the simultaneously born ego, the inborn ego. It is because it is so instinctive that it is so difficult to catch its projections.

For this reason, we need a clean-clear state of consciousness gained first from concentrating on the clarity of our mind; then we can cut the superstitious thoughts, go beyond ego, and discover mahamudra.

9

Now, Seek the Self and Find Mahamudra

Having become familiar with contemplating the clarity of our mind—as the root text says, "an amazingly skillful method establishing stillness of the mind and a way to introduce the conventional mind"—we can now move to investigate the wrong view of ego, how the ego perceives, so that we can realize mahamudra, our ultimate nature.

In order to experience mahamudra, we need to destroy ego's conception, the hallucinated idealistic picture, the concrete view, "this is *me*." So let's investigate this mistaken concept—because if we can't recognize how ego-mind projects its hallucination onto reality, our mahamudra meditation will become Mickey Mouse meditation.

It is very difficult to recognize the self-entity that ego is holding—that is why we first calm down the grosser levels of mind in concentration meditation. Without this concentration, there is no way we can identify the unconscious levels of ego holding the independent self, and therefore no way we can realize mahamudra.

Normally our sense of self is just a vague notion, and our ordinary superficial mind never attempts to pinpoint it. So we must investigate deeply and try to identify exactly how we think this fantasy I exists.

Lama Tsongkhapa says that if you're afraid of a snake but someone tells you that there is no elephant there, what good is that? Your problem is the snake! So we must identify the problem exactly; we have to make sure we understand clean-clear how ego holds its nonsense.

The Mindfulness Fish

So, let's meditate on mahamudra. First, achieve a level of concentration that you are satisfied with, focusing on the clarity of your consciousness. This is not something I can pinpoint for you, saying it's exactly this or that. But perhaps we could say it's when you've had a couple of minutes without emotional distraction—actually, that would be super! And be satisfied with that. Don't think, "Ah, only two minutes! I should be able to concentrate for twenty-four hours!" Don't grasp, otherwise you'll lose everything.

Then, from this clean-clear state and without distraction, move to investigate the opposite of mahamudra wisdom: the intuitive ego, our so-called simultaneously born ego. In his root text, the Panchen Lama says that you have to be like a fish moving through water without disturbing it:

From within that very state of earlier equipoise, in-vestigate intelligently with subtle awareness the essence of the individual who is meditating, just like a small fish that moves in lucid waters without causing any disturbance.

The main meditation, then, is strong concentration on the clarity of your mind. While you're doing this, your subtle analytical wisdom, your mindfulness fish, watches intently, ready to *capture* the way that ego-mind perceives the self-existent I and simultaneously *comprehend* the non–self-existent I.

Do not think that because you are attempting to concentrate on the mind you can't at the same time have another part of your mind be aware, be watching. For example, as you sit meditating you still notice the sounds of the breathing of others, the movement in the room, but you don't get distracted, do you? This is natural.

In the Tibetan texts they use the example of two people having a conversation while they're going for a walk—"A long way to go, baby!" There is awareness of the road, but they're not *watching* the road, not thinking that it's a good road or a bad road.

And don't think that the mindfulness fish is separate, like a separate thought; it's not. Yes, one part of your mind just keeps going, concentrating on the clarity, while another part, the mindfulness fish, watches intently; they do have different functions. Initially you experience them as separate, but as you learn to let go, you will experience them as unified. Just as the rays from a light that shines on everything are part of the light, so your thoughts are part of the consciousness that oversees everything.

Ego Is Like a Thief

What might happen is that the appearance of ego will come, but you'll miss it. It is like a thief who sneaks up when you're not looking and hides when you turn around. If you try too hard to find him, he disappears. This is exactly how ego-mind deceives us. It is so sneaky, so intelligent.

Instead of building up the strength of the ego, build up the strength of the mindfulness fish to catch the ego. Ego-mind is saying, "self-existent I, self-existent I," but your subtle wisdom is trying to recognize "non–self-existent I, non–self-existent I."

A Grosser Level of Ego's Views

If there is a real I existing, then what is it? You have to search. This view of ego has many levels, some grosser and some subtler.

The I is the body? You will experience many things, Lama Je Tsongkhapa says. Sometimes you feel that the I is somewhere among the aggregates, in particular the body. Superficially it seems that way. This body is the basis of our identity, isn't it? Especially in the West, the body is emphasized, so ego-mind strongly believes the essential self is related to the body.

So check, use your mindfulness fish. Is it in the nose, the ear, the other parts of your body? Is it inside the cells, the atoms? Ego thinks something must be here. "Somewhere in this body *I* am existing."

Sometimes you will feel this concrete sense of I in your heart; sometimes it seems to be in your chest, other times in your head. Or sometimes you might feel complete darkness, or you'll feel you're totally in space.

The I is the mind? The combination? Now think, "No, not only this body; maybe my mind is my I. Or maybe the I is one part of the consciousness? The subtle consciousness? My thoughts?"

Then, with more analysis, check to see if the self is the combination of the body and mind. "Maybe the combination of my body and mind is *me.*"

Keep your focus on the clarity of your consciousness. The mindfulness fish watches intently, without disturbing the clarity.

These are ego-mind's views, but they are on the grosser level. You have not yet discovered the projection of your simultaneously born ego.

You will see that ego-mind's object is *not* the five-aggregates body, *not* the mind, and *not* the combination: these are not what ego holds. These are not ego's problem. No.

Yet it's not enough to think, "The I is *not* my body, *not* my mind, *not* the combination."

Nor is it enough merely to *not* have the appearance of the body as me, the mind as me, the combination as me. The disappearance of that kind of impression is not enough to realize emptiness.

Maybe you have the experience of going beyond your body, almost a feeling of no-subject, no-object. That is good. But it is not enough.

Perhaps you have some view of what you think the self is—"Maybe I am this?"—and then you discover that view is not true—"I'm not this." This is not the realization of emptiness.

These experiences are *good*. But you haven't yet identified the nuclear energy of ego, the self-existent I, which doesn't exist but which produces all the problems.

Refuting these ideas is not enough to go beyond ego, not enough to discover the great seal of mahamudra. It's the beginning, but it's not enough. The appearance of the real I is more subtle.

Now Investigate Ego's Real View

Go more deeply. Check carefully. Stay focused on the clarity of your mind. Move the mindfulness fish without disturbing the clarity; it watches intently. It is ready to capture the conception of ego.

What ego-mind is *really* holding is an I that exists from itself. It *totally* believes that somewhere, *somewhere* deep inside you, solidly within you, *beyond* the body, *beyond* the mind, there is the concrete identification "me."

It is something that is quite unrelated, that is not dependent, that is not an interdependent phenomenon—that is not dependent *especially* on the name "I," "self."

This feeling of an unrelated, independent, concrete, *un*-movable, *un*shakable self-entity *me*, an essential energy here *somewhere*—"This is *me!*"—is so deeply rooted; it's instinctive, spontaneous, beyond intellect.

And it's continuously there. It doesn't matter whether you're asleep, awake, talking with others, on your own, or even if you forget yourself: ego continuously holds this concrete entity I.

Even if you imagine someone cutting your body into pieces until there's nothing left, you'll still feel that there's an independent, unrelated I there. This is so intuitive, so spontaneous.

So, with your mindfulness fish, watch for that I, the I that exists from itself, without depending on the name, that goes beyond your relative characteristics. Try to identify this I that you totally believe exists somewhere *here*—the real I, the real self.

This is *difficult*. It is not easy to catch this projection of the simultaneously born ego. You need sharp wisdom. Sometimes it will come, but you will miss it, so your mindfulness fish must watch intently.

Do not conceptualize. Keep the focus on the natural experience of your universal consciousness. You experience peace, joy, bliss.

Without moving the ocean of your mind, use your mindfulness fish.

For a moment it might catch ego-mind holding the objectively existent I, which appears to exist without label, without name, without any circumstances—and *then* for a moment it will discover that such an entity is totally *non*existent. Your subtle wisdom comprehends nonduality I, non–self-existent I.

Experience the selflessness. Let go.

Again the intuitive ego view will come, and again you will feel that the I is there. Again penetrate, and again it will disappear and an experience of nonduality will come.

Each time you find the *non*existence of your I, you are experiencing nonduality. Contemplate. Leave your mind in that state.

Look for Your Self-Existent Neighbor

Now, without opening your eyes, reach out and touch the person sitting next to you with your hand. Touch their lap, their arm, whatever. Just reach out and touch them, don't open your eyes.

Keep your awareness on the clarity of your own consciousness, but at the same time check: Is your neighbor existing from their own side, or not?

Are you touching a self-existent neighbor? One that you feel is already existing there before you touched them? Or are you touching only your superstition's projection, existing only in name?

Use your mindfulness fish to investigate.

Maybe you feel that you are touching a self-existent person, one that is objectively existent. Your uncontrolled ego holds such an entity—so out of control that you almost feel that you have to rush off to see your girlfriend, your boyfriend!

You feel your neighbor is already *there*, solid, separately existing. Your hand is touching someone that does not depend upon the label, having nothing to do with you calling them "neighbor."

Keep your intense awareness stable on the clarity of your mind, use your mindfulness fish. Is your hand touching a self-existent entity? Self-existent neighbor? Self-existent bone, blood, skin?

Like in a Dream

Let's use an example. Say that you dream of ladies and gentlemen enjoying things; they are dream people and dream enjoyments, aren't they? They come from your sleeping mind. They are real as long as you are dreaming. This reality of people and pleasures is a projection of your mind, totally coming from your consciousness.

They are not objectively existent in themselves; there are no objectively self-existent ladies and gentlemen or experiences of pleasure; there aren't. They are only hallucinated dream-mind experiences. As long as you are in that dream state, they will feel true. But when you wake up, they are seen to be nonexistent. You know that the dream people are not reality; they don't exist as you perceived them.

Well, it's the same with our neighbor; this is a perfect example. We feel that my dear friend who is sitting next to me today is the same as yesterday's friend. We believe that the neighbor I touch today was already *there*.

If I ask you, "Is yesterday's neighbor still existing?" you will say no, because intellectually we understand that yesterday's object is not existing today. We *know* that things change moment by moment. But when we touch our neighbor now, we think that yesterday's neighbor is *there* today.

My point is: whether it's dream-state or waking-state ladies and gentlemen, or whatever phenomenon in the sensory world, they are *not* existing from themselves. They manifest from our consciousness; they are labeled by our superstitions.

Lose the Self-Existent Neighbor

With your mindfulness fish, *discover* that there is no self-existent neighbor, a neighbor existing in themselves. What you touch with your hand is a non–self-existent neighbor.

Your neighbor does not exist within themselves; they are manifesting from your mind, they are labeled by your superstitions. Your own concepts make up your neighbor.

When the concepts disappear, the object also disappears, because object and subject are interdependent. The dualistic mandala has collapsed. You experience nonduality.

Contemplate this.

Lose the Self-Existent Self

It's the same with your own self: "*I* touch the other." Keep your awareness on the clarity of your consciousness.

Again, your mindfulness fish watches intently, checking how ego-mind holds the self: this deepest nature, this concrete, unconnected, solid entity, *somewhere* deep inside.

This time, the intuitive mindfulness fish captures ego's concept—and then it *discovers* that the I that appears to exist from itself, without depending on anything, not one dependent particle, does not exist as it appears, is totally nonexistent within any phenomenon, internally or externally.

The view of the simultaneously born ego that holds such a projection of ego—the concept of I, the fantasy that you have built up—dissolves. You the seeker and the thing being sought dissolve; subject and object dissolve.

That is the *experience.*

You might be scared! This is a natural reaction. For so long you have believed in this projection of ego, this simultaneously born ego, this built-up fantasy, so when it dissolves, of *course* fear will come.

During one of Lama Tsongkhapa's teachings on emptiness, he saw that one of his chief disciples, a great yogi, suddenly grabbed himself. He knew this meant that the yogi had experienced the loss of his I, his concrete sense of self. For him, the whole universe had gone, his self had gone. He was scared, so he grabbed himself to make sure he was still there!

Don't be afraid. It is conventional. Leave it, let go. Experience this non-subjective, non-objective state of consciousness.

There Is Nothing That Isn't Labeled by Your Mind

These are just my intellectual words. You have to capture this in your meditation with your intuitive mindfulness fish, again and again. When you penetrate, the sense of the self-existent I disappears. That is the real mahamudra experience. You discover the emptiness of the non–self-existent I, the non-absolute I, the I that is totally not existing in any part of your aggregates, the I that does not exist without depending on any circumstances, in particular without depending on your mind labeling "I." You recognize, as Lama Je Tsongkhapa and Nagarjuna show, that you exist *only* in name; there is no self-character.

This is a difficult point. To get the experience of this is not easy. Comparatively speaking, it's easy to concentrate on the clarity of your consciousness. That's *easy*. But it's not easy to catch the experience of ego. It appears suddenly, without your expecting it, so you have to be ready. Otherwise, as we discussed, you will miss it. It'll disappear, and then it's too late. Only afterward do we think of the solution.

I wanted you to experience this point with the person next to you, too; to notice that when you touched them, you felt that there was a person *there*, existing from themselves, something solid there, a self-existent neighbor, a neighbor that doesn't depend on your conceptions about them.

This is what we truly believe! If we think about that person, we can describe them relatively: they are this, that, with such qualities. But immediately we do this, we go too far, we go beyond normal. We go beyond what is there. We're not satisfied with the relative reality, with the conventional person. But it's not possible to find any absolute nature there. We should be satisfied with the relative. It's just the same as when we analyzed Scott.

Ego wants more, you see. It wants to find something there objectively: *here* is my friend! *Here* you can find the solid friend. No way! Ego-mind wants a friend that comes out from itself, someone definitely there that is not dependent on anything, that exists without depending on any other phenomenon, especially the name, the label, which comes from our mind. *That's* ego's conception.

The fact is, as long as the relative mind is open, the five sense objects exist, but when the relative mind disappears, the objects don't exist. When we are not using our perception, they are not real for us. In this way we can see that subject and object are interdependent phenomena. The existence of the five sense objects depends upon the relative mind.

But normally we hold everything to be self-existent. This is an unrealistic concept; it has nothing whatsoever to do with the objects of reality. According to the universal reality of mahamudra, that's a wrong conception.

There is nothing that we experience in this world of the senses that exists without being projected by our mind, being labeled by our mind. No such thing can exist, even relatively— not to mention ultimately.

But we think there is. When we touched our neighbor, we believed there was someone already *there*, self-existent, separate from our conception. We believed there was some solid person there, that our hand touched someone concrete. This is a total misconception!

Subjectively there's no such neighbor, no such self; objectively there is no such neighbor, no such self.

Once We've Identified What We Think the Self Is, It'll Take Just a Moment to Realize Its Emptiness

Even with the most precise introspective wisdom, seeking the I in every atom of our body, in every part of our mind, or separate from the mind and body, we will discover just how difficult it is to recognize the self-entity that ego is holding.

But Lama Tsongkhapa says that once we have finally identified *exactly* this false conception of I, the projection of ego, it'll take about a minute—a second!—to discover its emptiness, that it doesn't exist. It's like turning on a switch: in an instant we discover nonduality, emptiness, mahamudra.

Of course, this is only possible through meditation, when we've achieved samadhi. It's absolutely impossible to identify the entity that ego-mind holds by using the intellect alone. Using the mindfulness fish is not an intellectual exercise. It is *experience*.

The strength of our nonconceptual comprehension of the nonself, of selflessness, contradicts the concrete concepts, just naturally. In order to break the concept of the self, we use the mindfulness fish to help us experience the self-existent I as no longer reality: to intensively experience mahamudra.

Go Outside and Search for the I

When you are receiving mahamudra teachings, don't just meditate while sitting during the sessions. During the breaks, while you're walking around outside, getting into situations, as you experience things moment by moment, bring your experience of meditation with you; continue to use your mindfulness fish to catch the I.

This is especially important when you're excited—either when something bad happens or when you're extremely happy—because the feeling of the self-existent I arises strongly then. By using the mindfulness fish at these times, you can catch the experience of the self-existent I before it overwhelms you and realize that fundamentally it doesn't exist.

In this way, you're practicing all the time: during the teachings, while you're meditating, while you're eating, while you're walking. This is very useful. It's as if your guru says to you, "Now go and look for your I, seek your I." So when you go outside, you just watch, checking the concrete conceptions of the I—is the I existent or not? When a situation brings up the I, you check. Is the I there?

This practice is very important. During the breaks between sessions, you just look. Ego comes this way, that way. Check it out, skillfully investigate. No way you let the ego out! Then you can capture the thief: the projecting ego.

I remember a story my guru His Holiness Trijang Rinpoche told one time. A lama told one of his disciples that today he had to go look for his I. The disciple took this very seriously, very literally, and so went running up and down the mountains, all over, this way and that, seeking his I. After some time, completely exhausted, he came back and reported to his lama, "I looked for the I in so many places but never found it." He was successful!

There you go: not seeing is the perfect seeing!

10

Finally, Realize the Emptiness of All Phenomena

Greet Your Delusions with Pleasure!

Sometimes you feel overwhelmed by ego when you meditate—sometimes huge ego comes. Or perhaps, now that you have experienced some clarity in your meditation because your unbelievable Mount Meru of projections has tumbled down, you will be shocked at the difference between this state and your usual deluded way of being, your usual hallucinations. "Unbelievable! I am so deluded!" Your emotions rise up spontaneously.

But don't be depressed. When you meditate on mahamudra, this can happen. It's actually good that the ego comes up, that you see your delusions. Take it as a realization.

On the other hand, you might be so overwhelmed by feelings of such peace, of such love and compassion, that you'll spontaneously cry. There's no logic for it; simply being in such a clear state of mind, the tears will come.

Or perhaps, after experiencing the super quiet, the super peace, the bliss of your own mind, when you go out into the world and hear people's normal conversations, it is like the sound of scraping fingernails! Life can seem like hell!

And Have Compassion for Others

What you can do is convert these experiences into bodhichitta, so much love, so much compassion for all living beings, especially those who are hallucinating, so deluded, who have such a big ego, who are not touching reality. When you're overwhelmed by ego's projections, by all this samsara within you, you can remember that it's the same for everyone. So much compassion will come. It's okay. Let go.

When you have had even a little experience of non–self-existence, you develop such compassion for those beings who have not yet discovered this profound universal reality. You can see how they suffer because of their concrete concept of ego, holding the notion of "I." Their need is so great; they have so much dissatisfaction.

Whoever they are, rich or poor, enemies or friends—it doesn't matter. They all suffer so much. How can you not have compassion? This understanding gives you even more energy to keep investigating your own inner nature, to increase your understanding of non–self-existence.

First experience emptiness, then love, compassion, and bodhichitta. We need both emptiness and bodhichitta: they help each other.

Without the Mindfulness Fish, You Just Space Out

The great yogi Lama Tsongkhapa said that in Tibet there were many meditators who didn't understand the need for the mindfulness fish, who totally spaced out, almost as if they were intoxicated, and thus never touched reality. Nowadays, too, many meditators think that the analytical checking by the mindfulness fish is unimportant, or that it's not possible to have the one-pointed experience of samadhi and to use the mindfulness fish simultaneously.

But Lama Tsongkhapa's point is that it is possible—and necessary! You *must* use it to analyze what's going on, not only to check out who is experiencing the self but simultaneously to check whether you're spacing out, whether the clarity is strong, and so on. With the mindfulness fish you can touch reality, you can comprehend the nonduality I and the nonduality consciousness. Without it, the meditator ends up spacing out, or goes bananas—*that* is the great worry.

Another problem is that some people meditate for the wrong reason: they have such an aversion to the mundane world that they reject everything and then have psychological problems. They go off to meditate and end up in a psychiatric hospital. It's possible.

Experience in Meditation Doesn't Contradict Conventional Reality

When you meditate you can reach a point where you have an experience of the nonexistence of the self, objectively and subjectively. But you can misinterpret this experience. You can easily get the impression that therefore there is no I, no good or bad, no samsara, no nirvana, no cause and effect.

In your daily life you are so wrapped up in the relative mind, the grosser levels of mind, the conventional mind, that just naturally you think that everything is *really* existing—like in the supermarket: all those existent things! And then in meditation this egocentric I gets a taste of the nonexistence of itself, and you have an emptiness experience, no conventions, no nirvana, no samsara.

You can easily become nihilistic because of this meditation experience: you think it contradicts relative reality, and therefore nothing exists. But having the experience of nonduality in your meditation doesn't mean that conventionally there is no self or anything else. There is! Cause and effect *do* exist, the four noble truths *do* exist!

When you stop your meditation and open your eyes, again you use your conventional mind, and again everything is there. But the relative I and relative phenomena are the truth *only* for the relative mind; they are valid only conventionally. The self and everything else is an interdependent phenomenon, appearing like a dream, like an illusion, but nevertheless functioning in its own way.

So don't be confused by this, and don't be afraid of it. Don't confuse the conventional and the ultimate. These two worlds do not contradict each other, even though you might think they do.

Anyway, the relative I and relative phenomena are already existing within nonduality space, remember? They're not separate from it. They already have the no-self character, the nonduality character, the inborn nature of nonduality, of selflessness. That is their original character. They have always had this.

First Realize the Emptiness of the Self-Existent I, Then Other Phenomena

Remember, even though we might comprehend this intellectually—that the self and all phenomena are in the nature of non–self-existence—everything we experience through our senses and our mental consciousness still seems to exist as it appears to us: dualistically. The minute we open our eyes, we perceive everything, including our own self, dualistically.

Panchen Lama tells us that eventually, having familiarized ourselves in our mahamudra meditation again and again as we have described,

> whenever you investigate in great detail the way any object of the six [types of consciousness] appears, the way it exists will dawn nakedly and vividly.

Then he says:

> In brief, do not grasp at [the inherent existence of] whatever objects appear—such as your mind and so on—and always sustain, with certainty, the way they exist. With such understanding, all phenomena in samsara and nirvana are united in a single essence.

You see, mahamudra describes the universal reality of all existent phenomena, not just the self. But in the beginning it's not important to describe the non–self-existence of external things. First we need to experience it in relation to our self. We need to eliminate the concept of ego, this unrealistic entity that has never existed in the past, doesn't exist now, and will never exist in the future.

Once we've achieved that realization, experiencing the emptiness of everything else is easy. Having discovered the nonduality of our own self, we will discover the nonduality of the entire universe.

Panchen Lama quotes the great Aryadeva:

> Whoever sees one entity
> sees all entities.
> Whatever is the emptiness of one
> is the emptiness of all.

11

A Glimpse of Tantric Mahamudra

Now the subject is different. We will discuss mahamudra meditation from the perspective of tantra, the Tantrayana. Panchen Lama says in his text:

> Tantric mahamudra is the mahamudra of Saraha, Nagarjuna, Naropa, and Maitripa. In it the clear light of great bliss is produced from skillful means such as penetrating the vital points of the vajra body itself. It is the quintessence of highest yoga tantra taught in the corpus of essential works of the mahasiddhas.

Shut Down the Tourist Agency

We can say that we have two types of mind: resident and tourist. All relative concepts are the views of the tourist mind, the visitor mind. According to tantra, the wisdom of the tourist mind is not enough to understand nonduality; we need to awaken our resident mind. It is "resident" because it's always there, going from life to life, continuously flowing. The Tibetan *nyugsem* means "always there"—our original mind, our fundamental mind, the mind of clear light. But it has no opportunity to function, no opportunity to perceive universal reality, because the tourist mind, the conventional mind, is overwhelming it.

So, tantric mahamudra meditation is the method we use to manifest the resident consciousness, our clear-light consciousness, and to transform it into transcendental blissful wisdom. To accomplish this, we need to silence the tourist mind.

The tourist mind comes because we have the tourist agency. It welcomes the tourists, doesn't it? The tourist agency functions through the eyes, the ears, and the other senses, from the feet up to the head. The tourist mind is energized, repeatedly producing superstitions and confusion, as we've been discussing. To prevent the tourist mind from coming, we have to shut down the tourist agency.

The Components of the Body

As mentioned, our body is a combination of the four elements. We also have a network of subtle "channels" that run throughout the body, including the three principal channels: the right, the left, and the central channel. Then there are subtle wind energies that flow in the channels. We also have various *chakras* along the central channel: at the crown, the brow, the throat, the heart, the navel, and the lower chakras. And we have the red and white *kundalini.*

Normally the wind energies flowing throughout the channels energize negativity, the various superstitious thoughts, because our states of mind are connected to the winds. We have a saying: "The mind rides on the winds."

In order to activate the resident mind, our clear-light mind, we need to stop the winds from flowing in the outer channels and get them to enter into and stabilize in the central channel. This, just naturally, stops the tourist mind, the delusions, from functioning.

However, because some channels are knotted up at various points along the central channel—the crown, the brow, and elsewhere—forming the chakras, the winds and the minds riding on them cannot enter. We need to open the chakras.

The Resident Mind Functions Naturally at the Time of Death

This process happens naturally at the time of death. First our gross body ceases to function, then the subtler levels of physical energy, the winds, gradually dissolve into the central channel. Once all these energies have ceased, the tourist agency has closed down. Just naturally, the superstitions of the tourist mind also cease because the wind energies they're dependent on have dissolved.

Now—*pam!*—the resident mind, the clear-light mind, which resides at the heart chakra in the central channel, can function. Because they have practiced, the great yogis and yoginis can now experience universal reality.

Yogis and Yoginis Achieve the Dissolutions in Their Meditation

But they don't have to wait until death to experience this. They can go through this dissolution process during their meditation and awaken their resident mind. With their profound concentration they can stop the grosser levels of mind and the associated winds, thus causing them to enter into the central channel and stabilize there. The tourist mind vanishes, and now the resident mind, the clear-light mind, can manifest.

You Must Practice in the Context of Deity Yoga

You need to practice all this in the context of deity yoga. To manifest yourself as a deity, a buddha, is a very important part of the practice; in fact, deity yoga is essential. First, of course, you need to do the preliminary meditations, as we discussed: guru yoga, Vajrasattva, and the others.

A simple way to do the practice is by way of the *Six-Session Guru Yoga,* which you commit to do when you receive an initiation in highest yoga tantra. At the point where Guru Vajradhara sinks into your central channel, you visualize the process that happens at death, as above, and then dissolve into emptiness. Then you contemplate silently.

At this point you could, if you like, use the sutra maha-mudra approach, as His Holiness the Dalai Lama has advised. Contemplate the clarity of the experience of your own mind unified with the transcendental clear-light wisdom of Guru Vajradhara. Just be aware of it, and let go, without intellectu-alizing "Oh, my guru is this or that."

Next you manifest out of emptiness as the deity. You can visualize yourself as Vajradhara, Vajrasattva, Heruka, or even Tara or Avalokiteshvara, or any other deity.

Inner Fire Meditation

Now you need to do a technical meditation in order to open up the chakras. For beginners, inner fire, *tumo*, is the best, during which you concentrate on the navel chakra. You can use the other chakras, including the heart chakra, but the na-vel chakra is the best for bringing the winds and mind into the central channel, and much more sensitive for growing wis-dom. Focusing on the navel chakra causes the wind energies to go there—in fact, whatever chakra you contemplate, the energy automatically goes there.

Next—as the deity, remember—you breathe in blissful white light, imagining it as pure energy coming from space, from the buddhas, from the bodhisattvas. Then you tighten your lower muscles and bring up the energy from below—you could visualize it as yellow. Focusing on the navel chakra, you also push down, holding the breath until it's difficult to hold any longer. Then you exhale.

Contemplating the navel chakra like this produces heat energy because the red kundalini, which is the source of heat in the body, predominates at the navel. This causes the white kundalini to flow from the crown chakra, which energizes bliss. Even if you hold for a short time, it can be *very* powerful.

The stronger your concentration on the navel chakra, the more strongly the energy comes—just naturally, all the energy is drawn into the central channel. And the stronger the energy, the more powerful the flow of blissful kundalini.

The scriptures say that you don't need to worry about whether or not the kundalini bliss energy will come; it flows down automatically. For example, if you put butter above and fire below it, automatically the butter melts down. It's natural.

Now your subtle fundamental consciousness, your clear-light consciousness, experiences emptiness, nonduality, simultaneously with the explosion of bliss. This is the union of super, eternal blissful experience and the comprehension of great emptiness. This is the the tantric experience of mahamudra.

Practice as Much as Possible

Now you have an understanding of tantric mahamudra—a rough understanding, at least. If you have received a highest yoga tantra empowerment previously, you are qualified to practice. You should do these practices as much as possible.

So I think that's good enough. That's all we can do for now.

PART 3

Living with Mahamudra

12

Make Your Human Life Profound

Be Practical, Enjoy Life

If during this time together you have had even a glimpse of mahamudra, even just an intellectual experience, then that is valuable. It's good enough. Actually, I think it's so simple. Sometimes I think the way Buddhism is presented makes it all sound so difficult, even more difficult than samsara, and then people get scared! Life is difficult enough, and now this!

It's a matter of just practicing as much as you can. Be practical. Enjoy your life. By practicing mahamudra you cultivate the skill to develop inner clarity and go beyond the world even as you go about your life in the world. You can make your human life profound; that would be super.

Mahamudra is simple. You don't have to believe in anything. It doesn't involve any Tibetan ritual. In your own home you simply visit your own reality, your own mind. You don't need to light incense or a candle. Actually, for me incense is the enemy! I prefer Western incense: perfume. So I don't want you to think that Lama Yeshe comes along and pushes Tibetan culture on to you. I hope I never push.

The main thing is to have a clean-clear awareness of your own consciousness. That is super, super. That's good enough.

Use Your Mindfulness Fish

The function of mindfulness is to help you be aware of what's going on around you in your life situations. You don't need to react all the time. As in the example of the two people walking, you need to stay focused. You notice what's going on around you, but you are not distracted by it. You just let go. You know what's happening, but you don't conceptualize it as good or bad. No! You are just aware.

You are learning to change your relationship with everything: food, clothes, people. You're changing your projections, which come from your conventional mind; the reality of your life manifests from your conventional consciousness.

You have to learn this, to practice it again and again. Once is not enough to lead to higher realizations. You need to practice repeatedly; then this view becomes indestructible.

See Life as Like an Illusion

Once you have developed more clarity, you don't get taken in by all the external objects. You see them, but you have the space to recognize that they are the false view of your fantasy imagination. You think, "Oh, I'm experiencing an illusion." Then, not having such heavy concepts, you don't create heavy karma. See all your activities as illusory, like a dream. Bring your experience of nonduality from your meditation into your life. Learn to recognize that everything comes from your concepts.

When we talk about nonduality there is the connotation of the experience of being omnipresent, of embracing entire universal reality. Feel that your nonduality I is embracing all universal living beings. Try to experience whatever is happening without too many concepts.

Sleep Peacefully

At night when you go to bed, just lie down, your body relaxed and your mind in a state of clarity and selflessness, and then go to sleep peacefully. Your sleep will be much lighter—as if it's meditation. Then even sleeping becomes profound, your path to enlightenment.

Think about emptiness before you go to sleep. Sometimes during sleep there can be hindrances, physical or mental, but Buddha says that meditating on emptiness is the great protector; no one can harm you.

While you are asleep it's possible to be aware of what's going on in the room; it's almost as if you're not sure whether you're awake or asleep. This comes from successful meditation. I think it's natural, not something special. It shows the beauty of human beings, that we can do anything: it's simply a matter of deciding.

Then wake up out of emptiness and go about your life, doing what needs to be done, all the conventional things.

Use the Pleasures of the World

When you practice tantra yoga, or any other wisdom, you can make use of the pleasures you experience, whatever their source; you don't need to stop having pleasure. You use it to develop internal peace, internal bliss. This brings you satisfaction.

I think you already understand the difference between sensory gratification and the pleasure you get from meditation: such satisfaction! Even if it is unconscious, on some level you know.

I believe that every human being at some point experiences the inner quality of peace, the inner quality of bliss, the inner quality of love. We *do* have these kinds of experiences. But we don't have them continuously in our practice, and we haven't integrated these experiences into our lives.

Don't Make Demands on the Outside World

When you have found your own clarity, you are more peaceful, and then you are satisfied. You don't blame, and you don't make demands on the outside world, you don't demand pleasure from other people. In fact, if the external world doesn't work for you, who cares! Somehow you are no longer afraid that you won't get chocolate because you've found your own inner chocolate. Like this, you liberate your mind.

The nature of this peaceful state, the clarity state, is love. There is no room for hatred energy. Love is soft, gentle, relaxed.

Of course, it's difficult to stay in these states, it takes a lot of practice. You need to habituate yourself. Then, when you are happy, when you are satisfied, you give good vibrations to others. It's so practical.

Remember Dharma When Things Get Difficult

Dharma should help you when things get difficult. When the Chinese Communists threw us out, Dharma was the only thing I had left. And I was grateful. Dharma was my food then. When we reached the refugee camps, the actual food, the dal and rice, was a disaster! Just the smell of it made me sick! It wasn't our habit to eat lentils, and we'd get dysentery. The only thing that helped was Dharma.

I was twenty-five. I'd spent my life in the care of others, first my parents and then my uncles in the monastery. I hadn't explored anything on my own. So it was a big deal for me to come into exile and face reality in the larger world for the first time. Dharma was the only thing I had left, the only thing helping me to persevere.

It's not as if all of you will discover mahamudra or become great yogis and yoginis. But I want you to be practical. In everyday life, when difficulties come, when you're confused, just go inside yourself for a couple of minutes, touch your own clarity, your own nonduality experience; remember your natural state. This is so powerful.

Look at the Sky

Sometimes it's good if, with intense awareness, you simply look at the blue sky. Well, not really *look*; rather, just experience the space, the infinity. And then you can bring this experience into your own consciousness.

Or look at the morning sun, or a body of water, like a lake; that's super. Just watch it, without discrimination. Then close your eyes, and clarity is there. This is good enough. Just keep the memory of the clarity of your own consciousness. This is a direct way, a quick way to cut the confused thoughts.

Read a Book

Dharma will help you, absolutely! Even a *small* experience is good enough—don't worry about some super high realization. Just be down to earth.

And don't always push yourself. If you don't feel like meditating by sitting in the right posture, then meditate lying down. Sometimes that can be good.

Or maybe you don't even want to look at your mind. That's fine. Pick up a Dharma book instead, read a few sentences, maybe a page. "Oh, I'd never thought about that before." And every time you read the words, new answers will come.

Remember, Buddha himself said, "In the future, when I've passed away, don't worry, I will manifest as scripture, as philosophy."

Talk to Your Dharma Brothers and Sisters

Sometimes it's good to come together with your Dharma brothers and sisters, to relax and talk. I would do that in the monastery. Every evening after the teachings on mahamudra, I would meet my two Dharma brothers. We would light the wood stove, make a quick cup of tea, then we'd go through the entire teaching, repeating the day's subject that we had heard from our lama. Each of us would repeat it, back and forth, and then talk about it as much as possible to make it clear in our minds. Then each of us would go to our own corner and go through it all in meditation. That was our routine. I enjoyed it all very much.

You can do the same. Or perhaps you and your friends can come together for just ten minutes of meditation; this can help you to relax. This is the beauty of meditation.

Or when you're feeling uneasy, you can call your friend. "Hey, what are you doing? Why don't you come for coffee?" Then you can talk and relax. We human beings have each other; we can give each other wisdom.

Be Harmonious

It's good that as much as possible you are harmonious with each other, unified. Personally I think we should never criticize each other. One of Buddha's best sayings is never to judge others.

Judging others is too dangerous! Shantideva says that being angry with a bodhisattva is incredibly heavy karma. Who knows whether someone is a bodhisattva? Who knows?

Right here some bodhisattva might be listening to my garbage words. It's possible!

Among your Dharma brothers and sisters, in your Dharma organizations, or any other organization or group, it's best therefore to control your words. Words can be garbage; they are the product of dualistic concepts.

If you can help each other, then do so. But if you can't, just be silent. Silence is best. Anyway, judging others is a waste of time! We have enough responsibility taking care of our own world. And it doesn't help; it's not logical. Sure, if it does help the world, then, yes, criticize, protest: do it for others. But if it doesn't help, stay silent. That's my philosophy.

And in this way you will enjoy your life.

Organize a Retreat

It is good to organize a retreat on mahamudra: one week, ten days, whatever you can manage. Look at Milarepa! He spent years in retreat up in the Himalayas on his own, living like a kangaroo. All he ate was grass. We couldn't live like that for even a week, but we don't need to. We can eat rich muesli; forget about grass!

Some people say that you're selfish if you go on retreat. That's a wrong attitude.

Help Others

Anyway, being a Buddhist doesn't mean you have to go on retreat to meditate. If your mind is not clean-clear, then you do retreat. If your mind is okay, then you can help other people, you can serve others.

You can help other people with meditation, with relaxation—business people, working people. Help them know how to work without aggression, without disturbing others.

You can explain how the mind works; it's not necessary to give all the sophisticated philosophy. Simplify things to adapt to society. Buddhism has so many methods, so many ways to help different kinds of people in different contexts.

You need to touch people, magnetize their minds. You can't force the Dharma on them: "Here is mahamudra. I'm going to touch your mind! Take this lamrim!" They will freak out! But if we show them some simple meditation, even that can be profound.

Give Up Other Practices?

Some people say that because mahamudra is so special you don't need to do any other practices. They think, "Great! Now I don't need to touch my clean body on some dirty carpet by doing prostrations!" Well, if you can meditate on mahamudra twenty-four hours a day, if you can sustain a blissful state, that's super! Then you're right. But who can do that?

We need to practice Vajrasattva, remember, in order to subdue the delusions, to eliminate obstacles. And we must develop compassion. These will lead to mahamudra. The preliminary practices are necessary in order to realize emptiness. We can't be arrogant, saying, "Now that I have received mahamudra, I don't need to do these other practices."

Be careful. Think about this.

We Will See Each Other Again

We could talk about this subject for a lifetime, but I think that's good enough for this time. I'm fortunate to meet all of you, and I have had a good time. Thank you to the meditators and to all the organizers for all their hard work, especially Ian's parents: they gave so much love. Let us dedicate the merit from these teachings to the welfare of everyone.

One last thing. Don't be satisfied with what I've talked about here. Develop your practice continually, go higher and higher. It's a long-term journey. Continue to take more teachings, to study, research, and practice.

I am very happy. You dropped everything and came here. Your heart is in the Dharma. What you're doing is significant: you're truly bringing Dharma to the Western world. Therefore, I thank you so much from my heart.

When you have difficulties, when questions come, you can write to me. I'm responsible! I want to work closely with you. The world is so small now—I'm not going to run away from you. And we will see each other again soon.

PART 4

The Root Text

རྡོག་གི་ལྷུན་བཀའ་བརྒྱུད་རིན་པོ་ཆེའི་
ཕྱག་ཆེན་རྩ་བ་རྒྱལ་བའི་གཞུང་ལམ་
ཞེས་བྱ་བ་བཞུགས་སོ།།

ན་མོ་མཧཱ་མུ་དྲ་ཡ།

ཀུན་ཁྱབ་ཀུན་གྱི་རང་བཞིན་ཕྱག་རྒྱ་ཆེ།།

དབྱེར་མེད་བརྗོད་བྲལ་སེམས་ཀྱི་དོ་རྗེའི་དབྱིངས།།

རྟེན་པར་སྟོན་མཛད་ཁྱབ་བདག་གྲུབ་པའི་རྗེ།།

སྐྱ་མེད་བླ་མའི་ཞབས་ལ་གུས་པས་འདུད།།

Highway of the Conquerors

The Mahamudra Root Text of the
Precious Genden Oral Tradition

By the First Panchen Lama Losang Chokyi Gyaltsen

[Homage and Pledge to Compose]

> *Namo mahamudraya.* Homage to mahamudra, the
> all-pervasive nature of everything!

> I bow with respect at the feet of the incomparable
> guru,
> the lord of siddhas who teaches the naked [state of
> reality],
> the indivisible and inexpressible sphere of the va-
> jra mind.

མདོ་རྒྱུད་མན་ངག་རྒྱ་མཚོའི་བཅུད་བསྡུས་ནས།།

ཞིགས་པར་འདོམས་མཛད་དགེ་སྟོན་བཀའ་བཅུད་པ།།

གྲུབ་མཆོག་རྣམ་བརྫ་ཡབ་སྲས་ཀྱི།།

བཀའ་སྲོལ་ཕྱུག་རྒྱུ་ཆེན་པོའི་གདམས་པ་སྟེ།།

འདི་ལ་སྟོར་དངོས་མཆུག་གསུམ་ལས།།

དང་པོ་བསྟན་དང་ཐེག་ཆེན་ལ།།

འཆུག་པའི་སྐྱོ་དང་གཞུང་ཤིང་ཕྱིར།།

ཁ་ཚོམ་ཆོག་ཚམ་མ་ཡིན་པའི།།

སྐྱབས་འགྲོ་སེམས་བསྐྱེད་ནན་ཏན་བྱ།།

སེམས་ཀྱི་ཆོས་ཉིད་མཐོང་བ་ཡང་།།

ཚོགས་བསགས་སྒྲིབ་སྦྱངས་ལ་བརྟེན་པས།།

ཡིག་བརྒྱ་འབུམ་ཚམ་ལྷུང་བཤགས་ནི།།

བརྒྱ་ཕྱག་གང་མང་སྟོན་བཏང་ནས།།

དུས་གསུམ་སངས་རྒྱས་ཐམས་ཅད་དང་།།

དབྱེར་མེད་རྩ་བའི་བླ་མ་ལ།།

སྙིང་ནས་གསོལ་འདེབས་ཡང་ཡང་བྱ།།

Having condensed the essence of the ocean of
    sutric and tantric advice,
I will write down the instructions of the Genden
    oral tradition of mahamudra
of the supreme siddha Dharmavajra and his follow-
    ers, who give sound instruction.

This has three parts: preparation, actual practice, and conclusion.

1. Preparation

First, earnestly go for refuge and generate bodhichitta. Since these are the gateway and the central pillar of the teachings and especially the Mahayana, this should not be mere words.

Because seeing the reality of mind depends on amassing the collections and purifying negativity, first recite the hundred-syllable mantra at least a hundred thousand times and do as many hundreds of prostrations as you can while reciting the *Confession of Downfalls*.

From your heart, make repeated requests to your root guru, who is indivisible from all the buddhas of the three times.

དངོས་གཞི་ཕྱག་རྒྱ་ཆེན་པོ་ལ།།

བཞིད་ཆོལ་མང་དུ་འདུག་ན་ཡང་། །མདོ་སྒྲགས་དབྱེ་བས་གཉིས་སུ་ཡོད།།

ཕྱི་མ་རྡོ་རྗེའི་ཐེག་ཉིད་ལ། །གནད་དུ་བསྒྱུན་སོགས་ཐབས་མ་ལུས་ལས།།

བྱུང་བའི་བདེ་ཆེན་འོད་གསལ་ཏེ། །ཁ་ར་ཏ་དང་སྒྲུ་སྒྲུབ་ཞབས།།

ནུ་རོ་མེ་ཏྲིའི་ཕྱག་ཆེན་ཏེ། །གྲུབ་སྙིང་སྐོར་ནས་བསྒྲུན་པ་ཡི།།

ཀླུ་མེད་རྒྱུད་སྡེའི་ཡང་སྙིང་ཡིན།།

སྟོན་མ་རྒྱས་འབྱིང་བསྡུས་གསུམ་གྱིས། །དངོས་བསྟན་སྟོང་ཉིད་བསྐོམ་ཆོལ་ཏེ།།

འདི་ལས་གཞན་པའི་ཐབས་པའི་ལམ། །མེད་ཅེས་འཆགས་མཚོག་སྒྲུ་སྒྲུབ་གསུངས།།

འདིར་ནི་དེ་ཡི་དགོངས་པ་བཞིན། །ཕྱག་རྒྱ་ཆེན་པོའི་ཁྲིད་ཐོག་སྟེ།།

ཤེས་ཀྱི་རོ་སྟོང་བྱེད་པའི་ཆོལ། །རྒྱུད་སྔུན་ཀླུ་མའི་གསུང་བཞིན་བཙོད།།

ལྷན་ཅིག་སྐྱེས་སྦྱོར་གཉུ་མ། །ལྷ་ལྷན་རོ་སྐོམས་ཡི་གེ་བཞི།།

ཞི་བྱེད་གཅོད་ཡུལ་རྫོགས་ཆེན་དང་། །དབུ་མའི་ལྟ་ཁྲིད་ལ་སོགས་པ།།

སོ་སོར་མིང་འདོགས་མང་ན་ཡང་། །དེས་དོན་ཡུང་རིགས་ལ་མ་བཞིན།།

ཆམས་སྦྱོང་ཅན་གྱི་རྣལ་འབྱོར་པས། །དཔྱད་ན་དགོངས་པ་གཅིག་ཏུ་འབབ།།

2. Actual Practice

There are many ways to explain mahamudra, but they fall into two categories: sutra and tantra mahamudra.

Tantric mahamudra is the mahamudra of Saraha, Nagarjuna, Naropa, and Maitripa. In it the clear light of great bliss is produced from skillful means such as penetrating the vital points of the vajra body itself. It is the quintessence of highest yoga tantra taught in the corpus of essential works of the mahasiddhas.

Sutra mahamudra is the way to meditate on emptiness taught explicitly in the extensive, intermediate, and condensed Perfection of Wisdom sutras. The supreme arya, Nagarjuna, has stated that there is no path to liberation other than this.

Here I will give a commentary according to his intention and show how to introduce the nature of mind in accordance with the statements of the lineage gurus.

[Technique According to the Sutras]

Although called by many names—innate union, the amulet box, the fivefold, equal taste, the four syllables, pacifier, cutting off, great perfection, counsel on the middle-way view, and so on—when a yogi who is skilled in the scriptures and logic of definitive meaning and who has experience analyzes, all converge in a single intent.

དེས་ན་འདི་ལ་ལྟ་ཐོག་ནས། །སྒོམ་པ་འཚོལ་དང་སྒོམ་ཐོག་ནས།།

ལྟ་བ་འཚོལ་བའི་ལུགས་གཉིས་ལས། །འདིར་ནི་ཕྱི་མའི་ལུགས་བཞིན་ཡིན།།

བསམ་གཏན་བདེ་བའི་སྟེགས་བུ་ལ། །ལུས་གནད་བཅུན་དང་སྙན་བྱས་ལ།།

ཀླུང་རོ་དགུ་ཕྲུགས་དག་ཏུ་བསལ། །རིག་པ་དྭངས་སྲིགས་ལེགས་པར་ཕྱེ།།

རྣམ་དག་དགེ་བའི་སེམས་ལྡན་པས། །སྐྱབས་འགྲོ་སེམས་བསྐྱེད་སྔོན་དུ་བཏང་།།

ཐབ་ལམ་བླ་མའི་རྣལ་འབྱོར་བསྒོམ།།

ཕྱགས་དྲག་གསོལ་འདེབས་བརྒྱ་རྩ་སོགས།།

བྱས་ནས་བླ་མ་རང་ལ་བསྟིམ།།

སྐྱང་བ་བན་བུན་དང་དེ་ལ། །དེ་དོགས་ལ་སོགས་རྣམ་ཐོག་གིས།།

བཅས་བཅོས་གང་ཡང་མི་བྱེད་པ། །གཡོ་མེད་ཤུང་ཟད་མཉམ་པར་ཞོག།

བརྒྱལ་དང་གཉིད་ལོགས་ལྟ་བུ་ཡི། །ཡིད་བྱེད་བཀག་པ་མ་ཡིན་པ།།

[Seeking the View after Meditation on Calm Abiding]

Between the two approaches of (1) seeking meditation [on calm abiding] on the basis of the view and (2) seeking the view on the basis of meditation [on calm abiding], the explanation here follows the second approach.

[Sitting, Nine-Round Breathing, Refuge, and Bodhichitta]

On a seat suitable for absorption, adopting the seven crucial elements of physical posture, cleanse [the channels] with the nine-round breathing. At the beginning, with lucid awareness thoroughly release all impurities, and with a pure, virtuous mind, go for refuge and generate bodhichitta.

[Guru Yoga]

Meditate on the profound path of guru yoga and, after making hundreds of fervent requests and so on, dissolve the guru into yourself.

[Recognizing the Conventional Nature of Mind]

In that state where you are indistinct [from your guru] do not allow your conceptual mind to entertain any fears or expectations and enter equipoise without the slightest distraction. It's not the cessation of mental activity as when you faint or fall asleep.

Begin keeping watch with undistracted mindfulness and, with alertness, make your mind attentive to any movement.

མ་ཡེངས་དྲན་པའི་རྒྱུད་སོ་ཚུགས། །འགྱུ་བ་རིག་པའི་ཤེས་བཞིན་སྐྱོགས།།

རིག་ཅིང་གསལ་བའི་ངོ་བོ་ལ། །ཏྲིམ་གྱིས་བསྒྲིམས་ལ་གཅེར་གྱིས་ལྟོས།།

རྣམ་རྟོག་གང་དང་གང་སྐྱེས་པ། །དེ་དང་དེ་ཉིད་ངོས་ཟིན་བྱ།།

ཡང་ན་རལ་བསྒྲོར་མཁན་བཞིན་དུ། །རྣམ་རྟོག་ཅི་སྐྱེས་ཧྲད་ཧྲད་གཅོད།།

བཅད་མཐར་གནས་པ་དེ་ཡི་ཆེ། །དྲན་པ་མ་ཤོར་ལྟོད་ཀྱི་སྒོད།།

ཏྲིམ་གྱིས་བསྒྲིམས་ལ་ལྟོད་ཀྱི་སྒོད།།

སེམས་ཀྱི་འཚོག་ས་དེ་ན་གདའ།།

ཞེས་དང་གཞན་ཡང་ཇེ་སྐྱད་དུ།།

འཕྱར་ཕྱུས་བཅིང་པའི་སེམས་ཉིད་ནི།།

སྒོད་ན་གྲོལ་བར་ཐེ་ཚོམ་མེད།།

ཅེས་གསུངས་པ་ལྟར་མ་ཡེངས་སྒོད།།

རྣམ་རྟོག་གང་སྐྱེས་ངོ་བོ་ལ། །བལྟས་ཚེ་རང་ཡལ་སྟོང་སང་འཆར།།

དེ་བཞིན་གནས་ཚེའང་བརྟགས་པ་ན། །མ་སྒྲིབ་སྟོང་གསལ་ཧྲིག་གི་བ།།

ཕྱོད་བ་གནས་འགྱུ་འདྲེས་པ་ཞེས། །གྲགས་ཤིང་རྣམ་རྟོག་ཅི་སྐྱེས་ཀྱང་།།

མི་འགོག་འགྱུ་བ་ངོས་ཟིན་པར། །ཁྱུས་ཏེ་དེ་ཡི་ངོ་བོ་ལ།།

འཛོག་པ་རྟེངས་ཀྱི་བྱ་བཙོན་ནི།།

འཕྱུར་བའི་དཔེ་དང་མཚུངས་པ་ཡིན། །ཇི་ལྟར་གཟིངས་ནས་འཕྱུར་བའི་བྱ་རོག་ནི།།

ཕྱོགས་རྣམས་བསྒོར་ནས་སླར་ཡང་དེར་འབབ་བཞིན།།

Tighten by making taut and look nakedly at the nature of that which is clear and knowing. Recognize any conceptual thoughts that arise. Moreover, like a swordsman in a duel, exert yourself in cutting off whatever conceptual thoughts arise.

Having finished cutting them off, rest [your mind] and, without losing mindfulness, loosen by relaxing.

As it is said:

> Tighten by making taut, loosen by relaxing,
> and there is where you place the mind.

And:

> When mind bound in a tangle is relaxed,
> without doubt it frees itself.

In accordance with these statements, relax without becoming distracted.

As you look at the nature of whatever conceptual thoughts arise, they disappear on their own and a vacuity dawns. Similarly, if you investigate when [the mind] is still, a nonobstructing and empty clarity is vivid. It is called "seeing that stillness and movement are integrated."

Recognize as movement [of the mind] whatever conceptual thoughts are generated and, without blocking them, focus on their nature.

This is similar to the example of the bird that flies from a boat. As it is said: "Like the crow that flies off a boat and, after circling around it, lands on it again."

ཞེས་པ་རྗེ་བཞིན་བསྐྱངས་པ་ལས། །མཉམ་གཞག་རྡོ་རྗེ་གཉིས་ཀྱང་། །
མ་སྐྱེས་དངས་ཤིང་གསལ་བ་དང་། །གཟུགས་ཅན་གང་དུ་འང་མ་གྲུབ་པས། །
སྟོང་སང་ནས་མཁའ་ལྟ་བུ་དང་། །ཅི་ཡང་འཆར་བས་ཅིག་གི་བ། །

དེ་ལྟར་སེམས་ཀྱི་ཆོས་ཉིད་ནི། །མདོ་སྒྱུམ་ལྷག་གིས་མཐོང་མོང་ཀྱང་། །
འདི་ཞེས་གཟུང་ཞིང་བསྩན་དུ་མེད། །གང་ཞར་འཛིན་མེད་ལྷུག་པར་འཇོག །
འདི་ནི་སངས་རྒྱས་སྤྱར་བཅངས་སྐུ། །གཏོད་པའི་གདམས་ངག་ཡིན་ནོ་ཞེས། །
དེང་སང་གདས་རིའི་སྐོམ་ཆེན་པ། །ཐལ་ཆེར་དགོངས་པ་གཅིག་གིས་སྐྱོག །
དེ་ལྟར་མོད་ཀྱི་ཚུལ་འདི་ནི། །དྲང་པོ་ལས་ཅན་སེམས་གནས་པ། །
བསྒྱུབ་པའི་རྐྱུད་བྱུང་ཐབས་མཁས་དང་། །སེམས་ཀྱི་ཀུན་སྟོང་དོ་སྟོང་ཚུལ། །
ཡིན་ཞེས་ཆོས་ཀྱི་རྒྱལ་མཆན་སྨྲ། །

དེ་ནི་སེམས་ཀྱི་ཆོས་ཉིད་ལ། །དོ་སྒོད་རྗེ་ལྟར་བུ་བའི་ཚུལ། །
སངས་རྒྱས་རྣམས་ཀྱི་ཡེ་ཤེས་ཀུན། །དུར་སྐྱིག་འཛིན་པའི་ཚུལ་བཟུང་ནས། །
བདག་བློ་རྐོངས་པའི་མུན་སེལ་བའི། །རྒྱ་བའི་བླ་མའི་ཞལ་གདམས་དགོད། །
སྤྱར་ཀྱི་མཉམ་གཞག་དང་ཉིད་ལས། །མི་གཡོས་དངས་པའི་རྒྱ་ནད་དུ། །
རྗེ་ལྟར་ཉིའུ་རྒྱུད་འབྱུག་པ་ལྟར། །ཐུ་མོའི་ཤེས་པས་སྐྱོམ་པ་པོའི། །
སྐྱེས་བུའི་རང་བཞིན་མཇུངས་པར་བཅུག །

འཐགས་པ་སྨྲུ་སྒྲུབ་སྐྱོབ་ཞེས་ཀྱིས། །

སྐྱེས་བུ་ས་མིན་རྒྱ་མ་ཡིན། །མི་མིན་རྒྱུད་མིན་ནས་མཁའ་མིན། །

Having practiced in this way, the nature of any equipoise is a space of vacuity, since it is nonobstructing, lucid, clear, and unobstructed by anything material. It is also vivid since anything [can] appear.

This reality of the mind is indeed perceived directly with insight, but it can't be indicated, grasped at, or named as "this."

These days most of the great meditators of the Land of Snows agree that placing the mind in a relaxed manner on whatever dawns, without grasping, is renowned as "instruction kindling buddhahood."

I, Chokyi Gyaltsen, say that for beginners, this is an amazingly skillful method establishing stillness of the mind and a way to introduce the conventional mind.

[Recognizing the Ultimate Reality of the Mind]

As for the way to introduce the reality of the mind, I will record the oral instruction of my root guru. He is the pristine wisdom of all buddhas, who assumed the aspect of a saffron-robed monk and removed the darkness of my confused mind.

From within that very state of earlier equipoise, investigate intelligently with subtle awareness the essence of the individual who is meditating, just like a small fish that moves in lucid waters without causing any disturbance.

Arya Nagarjuna himself stated (*Precious Garland* 1.80–81):

The individual is not earth, is not water,

རྣམ་ཤེས་མ་ཡིན་ཀུན་མིན་ན། །དེ་ལས་གཞན་ན་སྐྱེས་བུ་གང་། །

སྐྱེས་བུ་ཁམས་དྲུག་འདུས་པའི་ཕྱིར། །ཡང་དག་མ་ཡིན་ཇི་ལྟ་བར། །
དེ་བཞིན་ཁམས་རེ་རེ་ཡང་། །འདུས་ཕྱིར་ཡང་དག་ཉིད་དུ་མིན། །

གསུངས་པ་ཇི་བཞིན་བཙལ་བ་ན།།

མཚམས་གཞག་མཚམས་པར་འཛིག་མཁན་སོགས། །ཧྲུལ་ཕྱན་ཚམ་ཡང་མ་རྙེད་པ། །
དེ་ཚེ་གཡེང་མེད་རྩེ་གཅིག་ཏུ། །ཉམ་མཁའ་ལྟ་བུའི་མཚམས་གཞག་སྐྱོང་། །

ཡང་ན་མཚམས་པར་བཞག་པའི་དང་། །གཟུགས་སུ་མ་གྲུབ་སྟོང་སང་རེ། །
སྐྲིབ་མེད་སྟ་ཚོགས་འཆར་ཞིང་འགྲོ། །འགག་མེད་གསལ་ཞིང་རིག་པའི་རྒྱུན། །
ཆད་པ་མེད་པར་འཇུག་པའི་སེམས། །ལྷོས་མེད་སྲང་ཞིང་འཇིན་པ་ཡི། །
ཞེན་ཡུལ་མགོན་པོ་ཞི་བ་ལྷས། །

རྒྱུད་དང་ཚོགས་ཞེས་བྱ་བ་ནི། །
འཕྲེང་བ་དམག་སོགས་བཞིན་དུ་བརྗོད། །

ཞེས་གསུངས་ལྡང་དང་རིགས་པ་ཡིས། །
སྣང་ཆུལ་ལྷར་དུ་མ་གྲུབ་པའི། །
དང་དུ་རྩེ་གཅིག་མཚམས་པར་གཞོག །

is not fire, is not wind, is not space,
is not awareness, it is not all of these.
Yet what individual is there other than these?

Just as the individual is not real
because it is composed of the six elements,
likewise the elements themselves are not real
because they are themselves composite.

When, having investigated according to his statement, you find not even an atom of the equipoise and the practitioner who enters equipoise, sustain a space-like equipoise, single-pointedly and without distractions.

Moreover, from within the state of equipoise, various [objects] appear and proliferate in this non-obstructing vacuity that is not established as material [form.] [Recognize] this non-obstructing continuum, the mind that engages continuously, as clear and knowing. The conceiving mind appears to not rely on anything else, and as for the objects it apprehends, Protector Shantideva has stated (*Guide to the Bodhisattva Way of Life* 8.101):

What is called a *continuum* or a *collection*
is false, in the same way as are a mala, an army, and
so on.

Relying on scriptures and logic, enter single-pointed equipoise in the state where things do not exist in the way they appear.

མདོར་ན་བདག་གི་དགེ་བའི་བཤེས།།

དོན་དང་མཐུན་པའི་ཐབས་ཅད་མཁྱེན།།

སངས་རྒྱས་ཡེ་ཤེས་ཞལ་སྟ་ནས།།

གང་ཤར་རྣམ་ཐོག་འཛིན་པར་ཡོངས་རིག་ན།།

དོན་དམ་ཚོམ་དབྱིངས་གཞན་ལ་སྤྲོས་མེད་འཆར།།

ཤར་བའི་དང་དུ་རིག་པ་ཞུགས་པ་ལ།།

རྗེ་གཅིག་མཉམ་པར་འཇོག་པ་ཨེ་མ་ཧོ།།

ཞེས་གསུངས་ཏེ་བཞིན་དག་པས་ཀྱང་།།

སྟོང་པའི་དང་དུ་རིག་པའི་མདུང་བསྐོར་བྱ།།

ལྟ་བ་ལ་ཐོགས་ཐུག་མེད་དོ་དེང་རེ་བ།།

ཞེས་སོགས་དགོངས་པ་གཅིག་ཏུ་གནས།།

རྗེས་ནི་ཕྱག་ཆེན་བསྐོམས་པ་ལས། །ཁྱུང་བའི་རྣལ་དགར་ཅི་མཆིས་པ།།

དུས་གསུམ་དགེ་ཚོགས་རྒྱ་མཚོར་བཅས། །བླ་མེད་བྱང་ཆུབ་ཆེན་པོར་བསྔོ།།

དེ་ལྟར་གོམས་ནས་ཚོགས་དྲུག་གི །ཡུལ་དུ་སྣང་བ་ཅི་ཤར་ཡང་།།

སྣང་ཆུལ་ཞིབ་མོར་རྟོགས་ཞིག་དང་། །གནས་ཆུལ་རྗེན་པར་སྣང་གིས་འཆར།།

གང་ཤར་དོར་འཛིན་ལྟ་བུའི་གནད།།

In brief, as my spiritual teacher, Sangye Yeshe, who understood everything in accordance with reality, said:

> When you fully understand that whatever dawns in your mind is apprehended conceptually, the sphere of ultimate reality will dawn without your needing to rely on anything else. Once you place your mind in the knowledge of that dawning, dwell on it in single-pointed equipoise. How amazing!

Similar to this statement, Phadampa Sangye also stated:

> People of Dingri, make the lance of awareness twirl within the empty state. The view is unimpeded and unobstructed.

These instructions converge in the same point.

3. Conclusion

Dedication

Afterward, dedicate whatever positive [roots of virtue] were created from having meditated on mahamudra, along with the ocean of your virtue collected in the past, present, and future, toward unsurpassable, great enlightenment.

Having cultivated your mind in this way, whenever you investigate in great detail the way any object of the six [types of consciousness] appears, the way it exists will dawn nakedly and vividly. Recognize whatever arises in your mind.

མདོར་ན་རང་ཤེམས་ལ་སོགས་པ།།
གང་གང་སྣང་བའི་དོན་དེ་ར་ནི། །ཨ་འཇིན་དེ་དེའི་གནས་ཚུལ་དེ།།
དེས་པར་ཀྱིས་ལ་ཁྲག་ཏུ་སྐྱོངས།།

འདི་ལྟར་ཤེས་ནས་འཁོར་འདས་ཀྱི།།
ཚོས་ཀུན་རང་བཞིན་གཅིག་ཏུ་སྟོར།།
དེ་སྐད་དུ་ཡང་འཁགས་པ་ལྟས།།
དངོས་པོ་གཅིག་གི་ལྟ་པོ་གང་།།
དེ་ནི་ཀུན་ཀྱི་ལྟ་པོར་བཤད།།
གཅིག་གི་སྟོང་ཉིད་གང་ཡིན་པ།།
དེ་ནི་ཀུན་ཀྱི་སྟོང་ཉིད་ཡིན།།

ཞེས་གསུངས་དེ་ལྟར་ཚོས་ཉིད་ལ། །ཚུལ་བཞིན་མཉམ་པར་བཞག་པའི་ངོར།།
ཡོད་མེད་ལ་སོགས་འཁོར་འདས་ཀྱི། །སྤྲོས་པའི་མཐའ་དང་བྲལ་ལོད་ཀྱི།།
དེ་ལས་འདས་ནས་བརྟག་པའི་ཚེ། །མིག་རྒྱང་བཏགས་ལོད་ཚམ་ཞིག་གི།།
བུ་བྱེད་རྟེན་འབྲེལ་བསློན་མེད་པར། །ཁྲི་ལམ་སྒྱིག་རྒྱུ་ཚུ་ཟླ་དང་།།
སྒྱུ་མ་ལྟ་བུར་དང་གིས་འཆར། །སྣང་བས་སྟོང་པ་མ་སྒྲིབ་ཅིང་།།
སྟོང་པས་སྣང་བ་མི་འགོག་པ། །སྟོང་དང་རྟེན་འབྱུང་དོན་གཅིག་པའི།།
ལམ་བཟང་དེ་ཚེ་མདོན་སུམ་འགྱུར། །དེ་སྐད་ཟླ་བ་མང་ཐོས་སྟོང་བ་པ།།

In brief, do not grasp at [the inherent existence of] whatever objects appear—such as your mind and so on—and always sustain, with certainty, the way they exist. With such understanding, all phenomena in samsara and nirvana are united in a single essence. Aryadeva confirms this by explaining that (*Four Hundred Verses* 8.16)

> Whoever sees one entity
> sees all entities.
> Whatever is the emptiness of one
> is the emptiness of all.

The [mind that] is properly placed in equipoise on reality is indeed completely free from elaborations with respect to samsara and nirvana, such as existence, nonexistence, and so on.

Once you have risen from that equipoise, when you investigate you see that although agents, actions, and dependent originations exist merely through being imputed with a name, they still undeniably appear, like a dream, a visual distortion, a moon's reflection on water, and a mirage.

When [for you] appearances do not obscure emptiness, and emptiness does not obscure appearances, the noble path of emptiness and dependent origination having the same meaning will manifest.

[Colophon and Dedication]

These words were written by the renunciate Losang Chokyi Gyaltsen, who has heard many teachings. Through this merit

བློ་བཟང་ཆོས་ཀྱི་རྒྱལ་མཚན་ཞེས་བུ་སྟེ།། དགེ་བས་འགྲོ་ཀུན་ཞི་སྟོ་གཉིས་པ་དང་།
ཐུལ་བའི་ལམ་འདིས་མྱུར་དུ་རྒྱལ་གྱུར་ཅིག།

ཅེས་ཕྱག་རྒྱ་ཆེན་པོའི་ངོ་སྤྲོད་བྱེད་ཆུལ་འདི་ཡང་། འདི་ནང་གི་ཆོས་བརྒྱུད་སྟོན་པའི་
བློས་གར་ལྟར་མཛོང་ནས། དཔེན་པའི་རི་ཁུལ་དུ་དྲང་སྟོང་གི་སྟོད་ཆུལ་གྱིས་འདུག་
ནས། ལམ་འདི་ལ་ཞམས་ལེན་སྙིང་པོར་བྱེད་པ་གནས་བཅུ་རབ་འབྱམས་པ་དགེ་
འདུན་རྒྱལ་མཚན་དང་ཅན་སྟོང་དགའ་བཅུ་པ་ཤེས་རབ་སེང་གི་གཉིས་ཀྱིས་རྩ་
མོ་ནས་ཡང་ཡང་བསྐུལ་ཞིང་། གཞན་ཡང་དེས་དོན་ཕྱག་ཆེན་གྱི་ཉམས་ལེན་
བྱེད་པར་འདོད་པའི་རང་གི་སྤོབ་མ་མང་པོས་བསྐུལ་བ་དང་། ཁྱད་པར་རྗེ་གྲུབ་
པའི་དབང་ཕྱུག་ཐམས་ཅད་མཁྱེན་པ་རྒྱལ་བ་དགེན་ས་པ་ཆེན་པོ་དེ་ཉིད་ཀྱིས།

རང་གཞན་ལ་འདོམས་པར་མཛད་པའི་ཉམས་མགུར་ཞིག་ཏུ་བཤེས་གཉེན་བརྟེན་
ཆུལ་ནས་ཞི་ལྷག་གི་བར་བཀའ་གདམས་ལམ་རིམ་ལྟར་གདམས་ནས། མཇུག་ཏུ་
བཤད་མ་ཐག་པའི་ལམ་འདི་མ་ཡིན་པ། དཔལྡི་གདངས་ཅན་པ་ལ་མ་གྱགས་པའི།།
ཕྱག་རྒྱ་ཆེན་པོའི་གདམས་ངག་མཐར་ཐུག་པ།། དཔལ་ཡི་གེར་འགོད་པར་མི་ནུས་སོ།།

ཞེས་དེ་དུས་དགག་བྱའི་དབང་གིས་མི་འགོད་པ་ཕྱི་དུས་ལ་དགོངས་པ། དཔེར་ན་
དམ་ཆོས་པད་དཀར་དུ།

བདས་རྒྱས་ཡེ་ཤེས་རབ་ཏུ་རྟོགས་བྱའི་ཕྱིར།།

may all wandering beings quickly become conquerors through this path that has only one door to liberation.

Having seen that the eight worldly concerns are like the drama of lunatics, Gendun Gyaltsen, with the degree of the ten fields of knowledge, and Sherab Sengye from Hartong, with the degree of the ten difficult subjects, live according to the conduct of rishis in isolated mountain valleys and take this path as the essence of their practice. They had already urged me many times to introduce mahamudra in this way.

In particular, the great Ensapa himself, the omniscient conqueror and lord of masters with attainments, has said:

> I have written an explanation similar to the lamrim of the Kadampas—starting from the proper way to rely on the spiritual master up to calm abiding and insight—in a song of realizations as advice for myself and others, without including at the end this path that has just been explained. I am not able to write down the ultimate instruction of mahamudra that is not well known in the Land of Snows.

What was not written down at that time due to restrictions was intended for a later time. This is understood by an assertion that is established, for example, by the statement in the *Lotus Sutra*:

> Since it is an object to be thoroughly realized by
> the pristine wisdom of a buddha,

ཐབས་འདི་རང་བྱུང་གིས་ནི་མཛད་གྱུར་ཀྱི།།

དེ་དག་རྣམས་ལ་ཕྱེད་ཅག་སངས་རྒྱས་སུ།།

འགྱུར་རོ་ཞེས་ནི་ནམ་ཡང་མི་གསུང་ངོ་།།

ཅི་ཕྱིར་ཞེ་ན་སྐྱོབ་པ་དུས་ལ་གཟིགས།།

ཞེས་གསུངས་པ་དང་འདྲ་བའི་བཞེད་པ་བསྐྱབ་པའི་ཕྱིར། སྟོན་པ་མཉམ་མེད་ཤྰཀྱའི་རྒྱལ་པོ་ནས་བཟུང་སྟེ་བདག་གི་རྩ་བའི་བླ་མ་ཐམས་ཅད་མཁྱེན་ཅིང་གཟིགས་པ་སངས་རྒྱས་ཡེ་ཤེས་ཞབས་ཀྱི་ཞལ་སྔ་ནས་ཀྱི་བར།   ལམ་འདི་མཛོན་སུམ་དུ་ཕྱགས་ཆམས་སུ་བསྒྲར་བའི་བྱིན་རླབས་ཀྱི་བརྒྱུད་པ་མ་ཉམས་ཤིང་།   དགེ་ཚིག་ལ་སེལ་མ་ཞུགས་པའི་རིགས་སུ་བྱུང་ཞིང་མདོ་རྒྱུད་དང་པའི་མན་ངག་འཛིན་པའི་སྟོང་བ་པ་བློ་བཟང་ཆོས་ཀྱི་རྒྱལ་མཚན་གྱིས། དགེ་སྦྱན་རྣམ་པར་རྒྱལ་བའི་གླིང་དུ་སྦྱར་བའོ།། །།

never tell those who take it upon themselves to
    write of this method
that you are enlightened. Why?
Because those who act as our refuge take timing
    into consideration.

I, Losang Chokyi Gyaltsen, who upholds the immaculate instruction of sutra and tantra and the undefiled stream of blessings of those who actually practice this path, have also become part of this lineage—starting from the unparalleled teacher, the King of the Shakyas, all the way down to my own root guru, Sangye Yeshe, who knows everything and sees everything. Without introducing impurities of samaya, I composed this text in Ganden Nampar Gyalwai Ling.

Glossary

absolute. *See* self-existent.

alertness. A mental factor, or state of *mind*, crucial during *calm abiding meditation*, that watches for problems, such as when *mindfulness* is weak, and helps get the mind back on track.

anger. *See* hatred.

artificial concept. *See* delusion.

Atisha (982–1054). An Indian Buddhist yogi and scholar, revered in Tibet, where he spent the last years of his life, whose *Lamp on the Path* was used by *Tsongkhapa* as the basis of his *gradual path to enlightenment* literature.

Atisha Centre. A Buddhist center in the state of Victoria in southeastern Australia, ninety miles north of Melbourne, affiliated with the Foundation for the Preservation of the Mahayana Tradition, founded by the author, and the host of the teachings in this book.

attachment. *See* desire.

bodhichitta. Enlightened attitude. The effortless and continuously present wish in the minds of *bodhisattvas* that underpins all their thoughts, words, and actions to (1) only benefit others and (2) never give up in their achievement of *buddhahood* for their sake, no matter how many lifetimes it might take. Cultivation of bodhichitta is one of the four *preliminary practices* required of the student in order to receive teachings on *mahamudra*.

bodhisattva. One who has accomplished *bodhichitta*.

buddha. One who, having achieved *enlightenment*, possesses (1) the effortless compassion to benefit all *sentient beings*, (2) the

137

wisdom—omniscience—that knows how to benefit them, and (3) the power to do so. When capitalized, refers to *Shakyamuni Buddha*, the historical buddha. *See also* bodhichitta; buddha potential; wisdom.

buddha potential. The natural potential of all *sentient beings* to become a *buddha*; the ultimate nature of the *mind*, its *emptiness*. *See also* conventional nature of mind.

Buddhadharma. Dharma, teachings. The teachings of *Shakyamuni Buddha*. *See also* refuge.

buddhahood. *See* enlightenment.

calm abiding (Skt. *shamata*). A subtle state of one-pointed, or single-pointed, concentration, beyond *conceptual* and *sensory consciousness*, during which the *mahamudra* meditator focuses effortlessly on the *clarity of the mind*, which, when combined with *special insight*, brings the realization of *emptiness*.

central channel. *See* channels.

chakras. Points along the central channel where various *channels* are knotted up. *See also* inner fire; kundalini; tantric mahamudra; winds.

Chandrakirti. The sixth-century Indian who explained *Nagarjuna's* presentation of the *middle way* teachings and whose texts are the basis of the study of these teachings in all Tibetan traditions.

channels. According to *tantra*, the 72,000 channels that, with the *winds* and the *kundalini*, constitute the subtle body. *See also* inner fire; tantric mahamudra.

clairvoyance. The natural capacity of the *mind* at a subtler level to cognize phenomena that *conceptual* and *sensory consciousness* can't, such as the past, the future, the thoughts of others, and so forth. A natural consequence of having realized *calm abiding*.

clarity of the mind. The conventional nature of the *mind*; the object of *concentration* in *mahamudra meditation*. *See also* buddha potential.

clear light. Referring to either (1) the natural purity, or *nondual* nature, of the *mind* or (2) the subtlest level of mind. *See also* dissolutions; tantric mahamudra.

clear-light wisdom. *See* wisdom.

concentration (Skt. *samadhi*). *See* calm abiding.

conceptual thoughts. Of the two ways that *mind* functions, *sensory* and *mental*, all mental experiences in day-to-day life—including *delusions*, such as *desire*, anger, and the root delusion, *ego-mind*, and positive states of mind, such as love and compassion—are underpinned by conceptual thoughts. *See also* nonconceptual.

concrete. *See* self-existent.

confused thoughts. *See* delusion.

consciousness. *See* mind.

contradictory concept. *See* delusion.

conventional. Artificial, superficial. The way that the self and all phenomena exist conventionally, that is, relatively, *interdependently*. *See also* emptiness.

conventional nature of mind. *See* clarity of the mind.

deity yoga. The tantric practice of visualizing oneself as a deity, a *buddha*. *See also* tantric mahamudra.

delusion. Artificial concept, contradictory concept, deluded thought, dualistic concept, dualistic puzzle, dualistic thought, fanatical thinking, fantasy, hallucination, hallucinated projection, hallucinated vision, impure concept, limited concept, misconception, mistaken concept, negative mental energy, projection, superstition, wrong conception. One of the three categories of *conceptual* states of mind—the others are positive and neutral—these negative states, such as *desire*, anger, jealousy, and the root delusion *ego-mind*, are the cause of the sufferings of *samsara*, but they are adventitious and thus can be removed. *See also* emptiness; enlightenment; liberation.

desire. Attachment, grasping. On the basis of the root *delusion, ego-mind,* a delusion that exaggerates the pleasant qualities of a person, event, action, object, etc., based on the false assumption that having it or doing it causes happiness, thus giving rise to expectation, possessiveness, and fear of losing it. According to the Buddha's teachings on the *four noble truths,* effectively the main cause of suffering in day-to-day life. *See also* samsara.

Dharma. *See* Buddhadharma.

Dharmakirti. Seventh-century Indian scholar renowned for his writings on epistemology.

dissolutions. According to *tantra,* the eight stages of the deconstruction of the physical and mental components of a person at the time of death, which culminates in the *clear-light* mind; *yogis* and *yoginis* experience these during their meditations. *See also* inner fire.

dualistic. *See* self-existent.

dualistic concept. *See* delusion.

dualistic puzzle. *See* delusion.

dualistic thought. *See* delusion.

ego-mind. Usually called ignorance (Tib. *marigpa*), this root, or main, *delusion* believes in the *self-existent* I and all other phenomena, which gives rise to the other delusions, and which is uprooted by realizing *emptiness,* leading to *liberation* from *samsara* and, when combined with *bodhichitta,* to *enlightenment. See also* inborn ego.

ego. *See* inborn ego.

emptiness. Mahamudra, nonduality, no-self character, non–*self-existence,* selflessness, totality, ultimate nature, ultimate reality, unity, universal reality. The ultimate nature of everything that exists—a buddha, a self, a thing, an event, an action. Because everything exists *interdependently,* it is therefore empty of existing from itself; the absence in everything of this impossible way of existing. *See also* ego-mind; liberation; special insight; wisdom.

enlightenment. *Buddhahood*, completeness, totality, universal understanding. The state that is achieved when a person has perfected the realizations of *emptiness* and *bodhichitta*. According to *Mahayana*, the natural potential of all *sentient beings. See also* buddha potential.

equipoise. *See* calm abiding.

existing from itself. *See* self-existent.

fanatical thinking. *See* delusion.

fantasy. *See* delusion.

fasting Buddha. Skinny Buddha. The depiction of *Shakyamuni Buddha* during his six-year strict fasting retreat, prior to his *enlightenment*.

five aggregates. All impermanent phenomena can be divided into these; here used to refer to the impermanent components of a *sentient being*: (1) form: the body; (2) feeling: pleasant, unpleasant, or indifferent; one of a group of states of mind known as the fifty-one mental factors; (3) discrimination: another of the mental factors, one that distinguishes one thing from another; (4) nonassociated compounded phenomena: all impermanent phenomena other than the above four aggregates, including the remaining forty-nine mental factors; often referred to as "karmic formation" or "compounded action," as well as "volition" or "intention," another of the fifty-one mental factors, because of its central role in sentient beings' experiences; and (5) consciousness: known as primary or main consciousness; *mental consciousness* and the five *sense consciousnesses*.

four noble truths. These truths for the noble ones, those who have realized them, was *Buddha*'s first teaching after *enlightenment*: (1) there is suffering, (2) there are causes, (3) there is the possibility to quit suffering and its causes, and (4) there are methods to do so.

Gelug. One of the four main traditions of Buddhism in Tibet, established by *Tsongkhapa*; the tradition of the author. The other three are the *Nyingma*, *Kagyu*, and *Sakya*.

geshe (Tib.). The title given to graduates of the study programs, which span some twenty years, taught in monasteries such as Sera, where the author was educated.

gradual path to enlightenment (Tib. *lamrim*). Tsongkhapa's step-by-step arrangement of *Shakyamuni Buddha's* teachings, presented as meditations to be internalized, based on *Atisha's Lamp on the Path*.

Great Perfection (Tib. *dzogchen*). A practice similar to *mahamudra* that is taught in the *Nyingma* tradition of Tibetan Buddhism.

great seal. *See* mahamudra.

guru (Tib. *lama*). Spiritual teacher. (1) The relative guru, one's teacher in human form, and (2) the inner guru, one's own wisdom.

guru buddha. *See* guru yoga.

Guru Shakyamuni Buddha. *See* guru yoga.

guru yoga. The formal practice of visualizing one's *guru* as one and the same as a *buddha*. One of the four *preliminary practices* required of a student in order to receive teachings on *mahamudra*. *See also* deity yoga.

hallucination. *See* delusion.

hallucinated projection. *See* delusion.

hallucinated vision. *See* delusion.

hatred. With *attachment* and *ignorance*, one of the three main *delusions*.

ignorance. *See* ego-mind.

impure concept. *See* delusion.

inborn ego. Dualistic self, ego, fantasy I, imaginary self, independent self, intuitive ego, real self, self-entity, simultaneously born ego. The self that appears to exist from itself, which doesn't exist but which ordinary beings, because of *ego-mind,* totally believe in. This belief has always been there, causing the sufferings of *samsara*, and is stopped by realizing *emptiness. See also* karma; self-existent.

inborn nature of nonduality. The self and everything else just naturally possesses, and has always possessed, the characteristic of *non–self-existence. See also* emptiness.

independent. *See* self-existent.

inherent. *See* self-existent.

inner fire (Tib. *tumo*). A tantric *meditation* technique for accessing the *clear-light consciousness* and achieving *tantric mahamudra. See also* dissolutions; tantric mahamudra.

interdependent. Dependent, dependent origination. The way that the self and all other phenomena exist *conventionally*: in dependence upon various factors, in particular the *mind* labeling them. The main logic to prove *emptiness.*

Kagyu. One of the four main traditions of Tibetan Buddhism. The Kagyu tradition descends from *Naropa* and *Milarepa* and counts *mahamudra* as one of its central practices.

karma. Action. The natural law of cause and effect that plays out in the minds and lives of sentient beings. Intentional actions of body, speech, and mind ripen in the future as (1) a type of rebirth, (2) a tendency to keep thinking or doing an action, (3) an experience similar to an action, and (4) an environmental result. Actions motivated by a *positive state of mind* ripen as happiness, and those motivated by a *delusion* ripen as suffering. For example, the action of non-killing will result in (1) a human rebirth; (2) the tendency to not kill; (3) the experience of not getting killed or of dying young; and (4) having a healthy body and living in a healthy, pleasant environment. *See also* liberation; samsara.

kundalini. "Drops" (Tib. *tigle*); one of the components of the subtle body, along with *channels*, *chakras*, and *winds*. *See also* tantric mahamudra.

lamrim. *See* gradual path to enlightenment.

liberation. Nirvana. Cessation of *samsara*. *See also* enlightenment.

limited concept. *See* delusion.

lineage lamas. The practitioners who pass on teachings or practices from one to the other in an unbroken line.

mahamudra meditation. "Great seal." A method for realizing *emptiness*. *See also* tantric mahamudra.

Mahayana. The "Great Vehicle." The teachings of the *Buddha* as expressed in the *Perfection of Wisdom* literature; the path traveled by a *bodhisattva*.

Manjushri. The buddha of wisdom.

Marpa. Eleventh-century translator and yogi, disciple of *Naropa*, and the main guru of *Milarepa*; founder of the *Kagyu* tradition; holder of many tantric lineages, including that of *mahamudra*.

meditation. An activity of the *mental consciousness*. There are two modes of meditation, named for their result: *calm abiding* and *special insight*. *See also* mahamudra; mind; sensory consciousness.

mental consciousness. One of the two ways *mind* functions, the other being *sensory*. At the grosser level there are *conceptual thoughts*, which include the various thoughts and feelings of day-to-day life. The subtler level is *nonconceptual* and is used in *calm-abiding meditation* to achieve the *realization* of *mahamudra*.

middle way. Free from the extremes of eternalism and nihilism. The middle way philosophy was articulated by *Nagarjuna*. *See also* emptiness; interdependence.

Milarepa (1040–1123). The ascetic Tibetan *yogi* and poet, foremost disciple of *Marpa*, famous for his intensive practice, devotion to his *guru*, his many songs of spiritual realization, and attainment of *enlightenment* in one lifetime.

mind. Consciousness. Defined as that which is clear (not physical) and knowing (capable of cognizing that which exists). Being beginningless and endless, it is not the handiwork of either a creator or parents. Mind is essentially pure insofar as the *delusions* are adventitious and thus can be removed. *See also* buddha potential; mental consciousness; sensory consciousness.

mind training (Tib., *lojong*). The term used to refer to the more radical methods for accomplishing *bodhichitta* as expressed in the practice of exchanging self for others (Tib., *tonglen*), popularized in Tibet by *Atisha* and his followers and having its source in the literature of masters such as *Shantideva*.

mindfulness. Memory. A state of *mind*, or mental factor, that enables a person to not forget what they're doing moment by moment. It's developed in *calm abiding meditation* and enables the meditator to stay focused on the object of meditation; it is supported by *alertness*. *See also* mindfulness fish.

mindfulness fish. The author's reference to the instructions in Panchen Lama's root text, "From within that very state of earlier equipoise, investigate intelligently with subtle awareness the essence of the individual who is meditating, just like a small fish that moves in lucid waters without causing any disturbance."

misconception. *See* delusion.

mistaken concept. *See* delusion.

Nagarjuna. The Indian scholar and yogi of the second century who, in presenting the *middle way* philosophy, clarified the meaning of Buddha's teachings on *emptiness*.

Naropa. The eleventh-century Indian yogi who transmitted many tantric lineages, including that of *mahamudra*; disciple of *Tilopa* and guru of *Marpa*.

negative energy. Negative *karma*. *See* delusion.

negative mental energy. *See* delusion.

nihilistic. The misconception that because everything is empty of *self-existence*, nothing exists. *See also* emptiness.

nirvana. *See* liberation.

nonconceptual. In general, not intellectual; specifically, a level of subtle awareness achieved in *calm abiding* meditation and used to realize *mahamudra*. *See also* conceptual thoughts; mental consciousness; mind; sensory consciousness.

nonduality. *See* emptiness.

non–self-existence. *See* emptiness.

Nyingma. The oldest of the four main Tibetan Buddhist traditions, which counts the *Great Perfection* as its highest practice.

omnipresent wisdom. *See* wisdom.

omniscient. *See* wisdom.

one-pointed concentration. *See* calm abiding.

Panchen Lama Losang Chokyi Gyaltsen (1570–1662). A guru to the Fifth Dalai Lama and author of the root text of the Gelug mahamudra oral tradition that is the basis for the teachings in this book.

Paramitayana. The "Perfection Vehicle." The *Sutrayana* teachings of the *Mahayana*. *See also* Tantrayana.

Perfection of Wisdom. *See* Mahayana.

positive states of mind. The states of *mind* such as love, compassion, and *wisdom* that, according to *Buddha*, are at the core of all *sentient beings* and are perfected when they have achieved *enlightenment*. *See also* delusion.

preliminary practices. Practices that prepare a person's mind to receive higher teachings. The four preliminaries to *mahamudra* practice are *bodhichitta*, *guru yoga*, *refuge*, and *Vajrasattva*.

pristine wisdom. *See* wisdom

projection. *See* delusion.

realization. A *nonconceptual* understanding of any one of the points of the path to *enlightenment*. *See also* calm abiding.

refuge. Reliance on the *Buddha, Dharma,* and *Sangha;* one of the four *preliminary practices* required of the student in order to receive *mahamudra* teachings.

relative. *See* interdependent.

renunciation. The giving up of the sufferings of *samsara* and their causes: *karma* and *delusions.*

root guru. One's main *guru.*

root tantric vow. *See* vows.

Sakya. One of the four primary lineages of Tibetan Buddhism.

samadhi. *See* concentration.

samaya. A practitioner's commitment to their *guru* to keep their word of honor or agreement to do certain practices, including to keep their *vows.*

samsara. Cycle of existence. *Sentient beings* are compelled to circle through the realms of samsara as long as they are bound by *delusions* and *karma:* the form realm, formless realm, and desire realm. The desire realm, in turn, has six types of beings: gods, demigods, human beings, animals, spirits, and hell beings.

Sangha. Spiritual community. The third object of *refuge.*

self-cherishing. Selfish.

self-existent. Absolute, concrete, dualistic, existing from itself, independent, inherent. The false way that the self and all other phenomena appear to exist, that is, independent of other factors, in particular the mind labeling them. *See also* ego-mind; emptiness; inborn ego.

selflessness. *See* emptiness.

sensory consciousness. The part of *mind* that functions through the medium of the five senses to cognize their objects, such as sound, smell, taste, etc. *See also* mental consciousness.

sentient beings (Tib. *semchen*, "mind possessor"). All beings other than buddhas. Those sentient beings who have not realized emptiness occupy the three realms of samsara.

Shakyamuni Buddha (ca. 563–483 BC). The fourth of the one thousand founding *buddhas* of this present world age, Lord Buddha was born a prince of the Shakya clan in northern India, renounced his kingdom, achieved *enlightenment* at the age of thirty-five, then taught until he passed away at the age of eighty.

Shantideva. Eighth-century Indian yogi and scholar of the Indian Nalanda Monastery, which flourished from the eighth to the eleventh centuries. His teachings—in particular his *Guide to the Bodhisattva Way of Life*—are revered by Tibetan Buddhists. *See also* bodhichitta; mind training.

simultaneously born ego. *See* ego-mind.

single-pointed concentration. *See* calm abiding.

six elements. A way of dividing up the components of a person: earth, water, fire, air, space, and consciousness.

special insight (Skt. *vipashyana*). Refers to the type of meditation for realizing emptiness and the *realization* itself. *See also* calm abiding.

superstition. *See* delusion.

Sutrayana. Here referring to the Mahayana teachings of the Buddha as contained in the *Perfection of Wisdom* literature.

tantra. *See* Tantrayana.

Tantrayana. Buddhist tantra. The most sophisticated level of *Buddha*'s path to enlightenment, entered into when a practitioner has at least a sincere appreciation for *renunciation*, *bodhichitta*, and *emptiness*. *See also* deity yoga; inner fire; tantric mahamudra.

tantric mahamudra. The realization of transcendental blissful wisdom achieved by the *yogi* or *yogini* who has accessed their *clear light* mind by practicing techniques such as *inner fire*.

Tilopa. Tenth-century Indian yogi and guru of *Naropa*; lineage lama of many tantric teachings, including those on *mahamudra*.

totality. *See* emptiness.

transcendental blissful wisdom. The *realization* of *emptiness* unified with bliss achieved by the *yogi* or *yogini* in practices such as *inner fire*.

Trijang Rinpoche (1901–81). Tutor of His Holiness the Fourteenth Dalai Lama and *root guru* of the author.

Tsongkhapa (1357–1419). Scholar, yogi, teacher, and founder of the Gelug tradition of Tibetan Buddhism.

ultimate nature. *See* emptiness.

ultimate reality. *See* emptiness.

unity. *See* emptiness.

universal reality. *See* emptiness.

Vajrasattva. A manifestation of Vajradhara, the form in which *Shakyamuni Buddha* manifests to teach *tantra*. The visualization of him and the recitation of his mantra is one of the four *preliminary practices* required before receiving teachings on *mahamudra*.

Vinaya. The Buddha's instructions on monastic discipline. *See also* samaya; vows.

vows. Formal decisions to refrain from certain actions of body and speech according to the three levels of teachings and practice: individual liberation, *bodhisattva*, and *tantra*. *See also* samaya; Vinaya.

wind. According to *tantra*, the subtle air energy that courses through the *channels* of the subtle nervous system that is inextricably linked to the various states of *mind*: it is said that "the mind rides on the winds." *See also* chakras; inner fire.

wisdom. In general, intelligence, knowledge. Specifically, the opposite of ego-mind: clear-light wisdom, omnipresent wisdom, omniscience, pristine wisdom—in other words, the wisdom in the *mind* of a *buddha*, which sees everything as it is and which pervades existence.

yogi. Accomplished male tantric practitioner.

yogini. Accomplished female tantric practitioner.

About the Author

Lama Thubten Yeshe (1935–84) was born in Tibet and from the age of six was educated at the Je College of Sera Monastic University in Lhasa. Not long after meeting his first Western students, in the late 1960s, he established Kopan Monastery near Boudhanath in Nepal. Here, as well as providing traditional monastic education for the local monks (and, later, for nuns as well), he and his main disciple, Lama Zopa Rinpoche, also taught courses and retreats for their foreign students. At their request, he started centers in Australia, the United States, and Europe and, in 1975, named this burgeoning group of activities the Foundation for the Preservation of the Mahayana Tradition. The FPMT now encompasses more than 160 centers, monasteries, projects, and services worldwide under the spiritual guidance of Lama Zopa Rinpoche.

Lama Yeshe's other books include *Introduction to Tantra, Wisdom Energy, The Bliss of Inner Fire, Becoming Vajrasattva, Becoming the Compassion Buddha*, and *When the Chocolate Runs Out.*

About the Editor

A Buddhist nun since the late 1970s, **Venerable Robina Courtin** has worked full-time since then for Lama Yeshe and Lama Zopa Rinpoche's FPMT. Over the years she has served as editorial director of Wisdom Publications, editor of *Mandala Magazine*, executive director of Liberation Prison Project, and as a touring teacher of Buddhism. Her life, including her work with prisoners, has been featured in the documentary films *Chasing Buddha* and *Key to Freedom*.

Also by Lama Yeshe

- *Introduction to Tantra*
- *Wisdom Energy*
- *The Bliss of Inner Fire*
- *Becoming Vajrasattva*
- *Becoming the Compassion Buddha*
- *When the Chocolate Runs Out*

What to Read Next from Wisdom Publications

When the Chocolate Runs Out
Lama Thubten Yeshe

"Lively and enlightening."—*Spirituality and Practice*

The Bliss of Inner Fire
Heart Practice of the Six Yogas of Naropa
Lama Thubten Yeshe
Foreword by Lama Zopa Rinpoche

"An impressive contribution to the growing body of Buddhist literature for an English-reading audience."
—*The Midwest Book Review*

Becoming Vajrasattva
The Tantric Path of Purification
Lama Thubten Yeshe
Foreword by Lama Zopa Rinpoche

"Lama Yeshe was capable of translating Tibetan Buddhist thought not only through language, but by his presence, gestures, and way of life."
—Gelek Rimpoche, author of *Good Life, Good Death*

The Mind of Mahāmudrā
Advice from the Kagyü Masters
Translated and introduced by Peter Alan Roberts

"Quite simply, the best anthology of Tibetan Mahāmudrā texts yet to appear." —Roger R. Jackson, Carleton College, author of *Tantric Treasures*

Mahāmudrā and Related Instructions
Core Teachings of the Kagyü Schools
Translated by Peter Alan Roberts

"This collection is a treasury of 'great seal' teachings from the most renowned gurus of the Mahamudra lineage, each text precious beyond compare. Every page exudes freshness of realization, holding the keys to our own personal awakening."—Judith Simmer-Brown, Naropa University, author of *Dakini's Warm Breath*

Essentials of Mahamudra
Looking Directly at the Mind
Khenchen Thrangu Rinpoche
"Makes the practice of mahamudra, one of the most advanced forms of meditation, easily accessible to Westerners' everyday lives. A wonderful way of bringing us to the path."—*Mandala*

Mahāmudrā

The Moonlight—Quintessence of Mind and Meditation

Dakpo Tashi Namgyal

Translated and annotated by Lobsang P. Lhalungpa

Foreword by His Holiness the Dalai Lama

"Has helped numerous serious Dharma students. It is excellent that the second edition is now being brought out."

—His Holiness the Dalai Lama

About Wisdom Publications

Wisdom Publications is the leading publisher of classic and contemporary Buddhist books and practical works on mindfulness. To learn more about us or to explore our other books, please visit our website at wisdompubs.org or contact us at the address below.

Wisdom Publications
199 Elm Street
Somerville, MA 02144 USA

We are a 501(c)(3) organization, and donations in support of our mission are tax deductible.

Wisdom Publications is affiliated with the Foundation for the Preservation of the Mahayana Tradition (FPMT).

LAMA YESHE WISDOM ARCHIVE

Wisdom Publications would like to thank the Lama Yeshe Wisdom Archive (LYWA), which provided materials used in this book. LYWA is the collected works of Lama Yeshe and Lama Zopa Rinpoche. In addition to archiving these lamas' teachings, the LYWA makes them available as published books and online. For more information, contact

Lama Yeshe Wisdom Archive
6 Goose Pond Road
Lincoln, MA 01773 USA